SALTED PEANUTS

1800 Little Known Facts

E. C. McKENZIE, COMPILER

BAKER BOOK HOUSE   GRAND RAPIDS, MICHIGAN

ISBN: 0-8010-5914-3

Printed in the United States of America

Sixth printing, January 1976

LITTLE KNOWN FACTS

- [ ] In 1894 there were only four automobiles in the United States.
- [ ] The normal temperature of a cat is 101½ degrees.
- [ ] It is impossible to sneeze when both eyes are open.
- [ ] Mrs. Dolly Madison, wife of President James Madison, was an habitual user of snuff.
- [ ] Identical twins are always of the same sex and blood type.
- [ ] Seven different colors are found in the human eye.
- [ ] At ninety degrees below zero, rubber becomes brittle as glass.
- [ ] When honey is swallowed, it enters the blood stream within a period of twenty minutes.
- [ ] Hummingbirds lay only two eggs during their entire lifetime.
- [ ] President Andrew Jackson was never convinced that the earth was round and not flat.
- [ ] Straight human hair is circular; curly hair is flat.
- [ ] Human blood is six times thicker than water.
- [ ] The world's tobacco spitting record is 24 feet, 10½ inches.
- [ ] Reindeer milk contains five times as much fat as cow's milk.
- [ ] In the Bible, a man by the name of Lot became the father of his own grandchildren. See Genesis 19:30-38.
- [ ] Crocodiles sleep with their eyes open.
- [ ] President Andrew Johnson learned to read and write after he was married.
- [ ] An expectant mother cannot "mark" her unborn child.
- [ ] Cut flowers become sleepy and wilt in the presence of apples.
- [ ] The oil used in fine American-made watches costs six thousand dollars a gallon.
- [ ] An ice cube will not raise the water level in a glass as it melts.
- [ ] The average American housewife opens 788 cans each year.
- [ ] A kangaroo cannot be led, but it can be guided by the tail.
- [ ] The male black widow spider is harmless to man.
- [ ] Daniel Webster's brain weighed 53½ ounces.
- [ ] By the time a whale has reached one year of age it has become as large as its mother.
- [ ] In 1913, the tax on a four-thousand-dollar annual income was one penny.
- [ ] Henry Ford forgot to put a reverse gear in his first automobile.

- [ ] The Irish language is the most difficult language to speak.
- [ ] Among the lower animals, it is the male and not the female who shows jealousy.
- [ ] Voltaire drank seventy cups of coffee every day.
- [ ] A chicken grows more than eight thousand feathers.
- [ ] Thomas Jefferson suffered throughout his life with migraine or tension headache.
- [ ] The tongue of a giraffe measures about eighteen inches.
- [ ] A man's heart beats eight or ten beats more each minute than a woman's.
- [ ] The normal pulse of a bull is forty-six per minute while that of a cow is fifty-six.
- [ ] Two former presidents, Thomas Jefferson and John Adams, died July 4, 1826.
- [ ] A stick of chewing gum contains about 8 ½ calories.
- [ ] The extended right arm of the Statue of Liberty is forty-two feet long.
- [ ] Benjamin Franklin was the first postmaster of the United States.
- [ ] A five-foot pelican weighing twenty-five pounds has a skeleton that weighs only twenty-three ounces.
- [ ] The engagement ring is still worn on the fourth finger. This custom originated because of the belief that the "vein of love" ran from this finger directly to the heart.
- [ ] A man whose normal weight is 150 pounds would weigh about 50 pounds if all the water in his system were dried up.
- [ ] No fiber feels so good next to the skin as cotton does.
- [ ] Amish men shave until they marry, then they grow a beard.
- [ ] Ninety-seven percent of all people offered a new pen to try, write their own name.
- [ ] The sweat glands of a hog are confined largely to the snout.
- [ ] Irving Berlin received thirty-three cents for the first song that he wrote.
- [ ] Hot water does not freeze sooner than cold water.
- [ ] A horse always stands with his rear end to the wind on a cold, rainy day.
- [ ] The sex of box turtles is determined by the color of their eyes.
- [ ] A dog is as old at twelve years as a man at eighty-four.
- [ ] Dr. John Witherspoon was the only preacher to sign the Declaration of Independence.
- [ ] Young salmon always swim downstream tailfirst.

- [ ] The popular belief that rain purifies the atmosphere is not true.
- [ ] There is no such thing as a living sardine.
- [ ] Spinach loses 50 percent of its vitamin C content within twenty-four hours after being picked.
- [ ] Cane sugar and beet sugar do not differ in sweetness.
- [ ] John Tyler was the first president of the United States to be photographed while in office.
- [ ] The male mosquito is a strict vegetarian.
- [ ] A horse, while trotting, has all four feet off the ground part of the time.
- [ ] The common house fly does not breed in Alaska.
- [ ] A young blue whale puts on weight at the rate of two to three hundred pounds a day.
- [ ] The color red irritates the nervous system. Green has the opposite effect.
- [ ] All the blood in the human body passes through the thyroid gland every seventeen minutes.
- [ ] A year on the planet Jupiter is twelve times the length of our year on earth.
- [ ] Saturday is the most dangerous day of the week to drive an automobile.
- [ ] Thomas A. Edison is believed to be the first person to say hello on the telephone.
- [ ] Four presidents of the United States were born in a log cabin: Fillmore, Buchanan, Lincoln, and Garfield.
- [ ] The heart of a snake is located about one-fifth the distance from its head to the end of its tail.
- [ ] It is not recorded in the Bible that Jesus Christ was ever sick.
- [ ] The fiscal year of the United States begins on July 1 and ends June 30.
- [ ] Both Julius Caesar and Napoleon Bonaparte were victims of epilepsy.
- [ ] For no apparent reason, men get appendicitis more often than women.
- [ ] Healthy pigeons have never been known to sleep or close their eyes.
- [ ] There are at least twenty-two hundred thunderstorms in the world at any given moment.
- [ ] Technically speaking, a pound of feathers weighs more than a pound of gold.
- [ ] Fish have the same number of scales during their entire lifetime.

- [ ] The Statue of Liberty weighs 225 tons.
- [ ] Treason is the only crime defined in the Constitution of the United States.
- [ ] A normal person has twelve pairs of ribs.
- [ ] Flying a national flag upside down at sea is a signal of distress.
- [ ] The "doodle bug" always walks backwards.
- [ ] Franklin D. Roosevelt and Theodore Roosevelt were fifth cousins.
- [ ] During the past four thousand years there have been less than three hundred years of peace.
- [ ] Sir Isaac Newton spent two years in the House of Commons (England) but opened his mouth but once.
- [ ] The eyes of an elephant are only slightly larger than the eyes of a man.
- [ ] A swarm of fifty thousand bees weighs about ten pounds.
- [ ] More than 150 different flavors of ice cream are now manufactured.
- [ ] James A. Garfield wore the largest hat of any president of the United States.
- [ ] German silver does not contain any silver at all.
- [ ] Rivers exist in the ocean as well as on dry land.
- [ ] The world-famous Dale Carnegie criticized at least 150,000 speeches.
- [ ] Fifteen million corncobs are utilized annually in the United States in the manufacture of corncob pipes.
- [ ] A camel can drink twenty-five gallons of water in half an hour.
- [ ] Whales cannot breathe under water. They have lungs instead of gills.
- [ ] Thomas Jefferson was never a member of any church.
- [ ] The largest snowflake on record measured eight inches in width.
- [ ] It takes seven thousand grains of aspirin to make a pound.
- [ ] The pressure cooker was invented in 1874.
- [ ] In the United States, a person dies every 14 ½ seconds.
- [ ] A bicycle built in 1898 could seat ten people.
- [ ] More than a quarter of a pound of salt is found in every gallon of sea water.
- [ ] A cup filled to the brim with coffee will not overflow if several teaspoonfuls of sugar are added slowly.
- [ ] The first appendectomy was performed in 1736.
- [ ] A Brahman bull purrs when he is happy.

- [ ] Andrew Jackson was the only president of the United States to marry the same woman twice.
- [ ] King Henry VIII was the most married English king, having had six wives.
- [ ] The longest fingernails ever recorded measured 23 ¾ inches.
- [ ] If a color-blind woman marries a man with normal vision, all of the sons will be color-blind, and all the daughters will have normal vision.
- [ ] Henry Clay had more nicknames than any other American politician.
- [ ] Dog sleds delivered mail in Alaska from the 1890s until 1963.
- [ ] The average American family of four eats more than 2 ½ tons of food each year.
- [ ] A violin contains about seventy separate pieces of wood.
- [ ] The nose of the Statue of Liberty measures four feet, six inches.
- [ ] Pigs were used in ancient Egypt to tread seed into the ground and thresh grain.
- [ ] Forty percent of the wounds caused by knives, guns, and ice picks are inflicted by friends or relatives of the victims.
- [ ] The record high jump for a flea is seven inches.
- [ ] A bird requires more food in proportion to its size than a baby or a cat.
- [ ] In the United States the railroad station bearing the shortest name is Uz in Kentucky.
- [ ] In 1904 the ice cream cone made its debut on the American scene.
- [ ] The ear is the most intricate, complicated organ in the human body.
- [ ] It cannot be proved by the Bible that Jesus Christ ever smiled.
- [ ] Henry Wadsworth Longfellow is the only American whose bust is in Westminster Abbey.
- [ ] The skin of a hippopotamus is two inches thick in some places.
- [ ] Two presidents, James Buchanan and Grover Cleveland, suffered from gout.
- [ ] On March 27, 1848, John Parker Paynard of Dedham, Massachusetts, originated medicated adhesive plaster.
- [ ] The average life of a spider is only one year.
- [ ] Birds take off against the wind the same as airplanes.
- [ ] In 1800, only about 7 percent of the population in our country were church members.
- [ ] The hawk is the swiftest of all the bird family.

- [ ] The first bank for Negroes was chartered at Richmond, Virginia, in 1888.
- [ ] Toads, in distinction from frogs, have no teeth.
- [ ] China was the first country to invent paper money.
- [ ] All snake eggs are white or cream colored.
- [ ] Oberlin College in Ohio was the first college in America to confer degrees of women.
- [ ] The liver, weighing from three to four pounds, is the heaviest organ in the human body.
- [ ] Dogs perspire through the pads in their paws.
- [ ] There are at least seventeen million hunters in America.
- [ ] Sixty days are required for a housefly to become a great-grandmother.
- [ ] President Franklin D. Roosevelt held his first "Fireside Chat" in 1933.
- [ ] There is no scientific distinction between pigeons and doves.
- [ ] Sound waves travel at the rate of 1,075 feet per second.
- [ ] In skywriting, the average letter is nearly two miles high.
- [ ] William Henry Harrison served the shortest term of any American president — one month.
- [ ] The jugular vein is not a vein; it is an artery.
- [ ] American consumers spend a billion dollars a year for cold relief preparations.
- [ ] Thomas A. Edison once spent two million dollars on an invention that proved of little value.
- [ ] A man's beard grows an inch in about eight weeks.
- [ ] The best jump a fish can make is perhaps five or six feet.
- [ ] Penicillin does not kill germs; it merely stops their growth and prevents their reproduction.
- [ ] A baseball can be made to curve 6 ½ inches from its normal course.
- [ ] In the United States a baby is born every 8 ½ seconds.
- [ ] A man has 20 percent more red corpuscles in his body than does a woman.
- [ ] Since 1959, it has been unlawful to shoot turtles in the state of Hawaii.
- [ ] A cubic yard of air weighs more than two pounds.
- [ ] Five counties in Texas are larger than the state of Rhode Island.
- [ ] Benjamin Franklin invented the bifocal lens about the year 1760.
- [ ] The United States is the world's largest landowner.

- [ ] Fish continue to grow until they die.
- [ ] The human eye can wink in one-fortieth of a second.
- [ ] Forty percent of the people of the world never have any "wisdom teeth."
- [ ] Presidents Zachary Taylor and James Madison were second cousins.
- [ ] In the year 205 B.C. the Romans passed a law prohibiting women from driving chariots.
- [ ] Cobalt was discovered by Brandt in 1735.
- [ ] It is possible for a sneeze to be of sufficient volume to crack the ribs.
- [ ] A hen that incubates an egg laid by another hen is the foster mother of the chick.
- [ ] There is no place on earth that is entirely free from electrical storms.
- [ ] Each day the human heart exerts sufficient energy to lift the body fourteen hundred feet into the air.
- [ ] At ninety degrees below zero, mercury becomes hard as steel.
- [ ] There are thirty-five known species of coconuts.
- [ ] The religion of President John Adams was based on the Sermon on the Mount and the Ten Commandments.
- [ ] All ants have six legs.
- [ ] James H. Doolittle made the first all-instrument flight in aviation.
- [ ] Seven suicides are recorded in the Bible.
- [ ] The first cheese factory in the United States began operation in 1851 at Rome, New York.
- [ ] Two hundred and seventy opossums, at birth, weigh only one ounce.
- [ ] The first ice cream freezer was patented on May 30, 1848, by Wm. G. Young of Baltimore, Maryland.
- [ ] Hogs eat any and all kinds of snakes.
- [ ] There are only twelve letters in the Hawaiian alphabet.
- [ ] The mouth of the Statue of Liberty measures three feet in width.
- [ ] In 1858, the first mechanical washing machine was invented by Hamilton E. Smith. It was a hand cranked affair.
- [ ] President John Tyler was the father of fourteen children.
- [ ] One ton of iron weighs three tons after it has completely rusted.
- [ ] The "funny bone" is not a bone, it is a nerve.
- [ ] Eleven hundred and fifty inventions were patented by Thomas A. Edison.

- [ ] The cow tree of Venezuela gives milk that looks and tastes like cow's milk.
- [ ] Often a duck swims while sleeping.
- [ ] The highest price ever paid for a stallion was $2,625,000, paid in February 1967.
- [ ] Ten inches of snow equals one inch of rain in water content.
- [ ] A strict Moslem man never takes more than five wives at one time.
- [ ] The bones of a pigeon weigh less than its feathers.
- [ ] A grown circus lion consumes about thirty pounds of horse meat each day.
- [ ] The highest recorded live weight for a turkey is sixty-four pounds.
- [ ] Key West, Florida, is the only city in the United States where frost never occurs.
- [ ] "Daylight saving time" was first suggested by Benjamin Franklin in 1784.
- [ ] Sheep were first introduced into the United States in 1609.
- [ ] Butterflies taste with their feet instead of their mouths.
- [ ] The oldest recorded age of a horse is sixty-one years.
- [ ] President Rutherford B. Hayes made it a lifetime practice to attend public worship every Sunday.
- [ ] The word *prejudice* is not in the Bible.
- [ ] Due to the earth's rotation, a shot put can be thrown farther if it is thrown to the west.
- [ ] The Jewish New Year never falls on Friday, Sunday, or Wednesday.
- [ ] A sick pig rarely curls his tail.
- [ ] The largest number of children produced by one mother is sixty-nine.
- [ ] From 1835 to 1837 the United States had no national debt.
- [ ] The aroma of coffee is not produced by the caffeine it contains. Caffeine imparts neither color nor flavor.
- [ ] Beethoven, the world-famous musician, composed most of his great symphonies after he became deaf.
- [ ] The "spread" of an ordinary parachute when opened is twenty-four feet.
- [ ] Thomas Jefferson was thirty-five years old when he drafted the Declaration of Independence.
- [ ] The people of Ireland are the greatest eaters of potatoes in the world.
- [ ] There are sixty-four hundred windows in the Empire State Building.

- [ ] Playing a game "according to Hoyle" means playing a game according to the recognized rules.

- [ ] The United States government paid two cents per acre for Alaska.

- [ ] One horsepower is equal to 746 watts.

- [ ] There are more than twenty thousand known ways of earning a living.

- [ ] The human heart stands still one-sixth of a lifetime.

- [ ] In weight, it takes thirty-two half dollars to equal fifteen silver dollars.

- [ ] There are 3,070 counties in the United States.

- [ ] The largest litter of puppies on record is twenty-three.

- [ ] A polecat and a skunk are the same animal.

- [ ] The evening temperature on the moon is below that of dry ice.

- [ ] Alcohol feels cooler to the touch than water because it evaporates at a much faster rate at body temperature.

- [ ] The "seventh inning stretch" seen at baseball games was first practiced in 1860.

- [ ] In a vacuum, all objects fall at exactly the same speed no matter what their shape or weight might be.

- [ ] The earth is traveling through space at the rate of 72,600 miles an hour, or 1,100 miles every minute.

- [ ] A tone is what you hear in music; a note is the written symbol of a tone.

- [ ] The expression, "blind as a bat," is unscientific. Bats have eyes and can see fairly well.

- [ ] In the United States one hundred persons die in traffic accidents to every person killed by lightning.

- [ ] The inside of a cucumber is often twenty degrees hotter than the surrounding air.

- [ ] Theodore Roosevelt was the only president of the United States who was not sworn in on a Bible.

- [ ] The federal government forbids the portrait of any living person to appear on a United States postage stamp.

- [ ] Synthetic diamonds were successfully produced for the first time in 1954.

- [ ] The average American family spends more than three hours each day reading newspapers.

- [ ] Benjamin Franklin could play three different instruments: the harp, the guitar, and the violin.

- [ ] The sound produced by the western meadowlark is the nearest thing to a chromatic scale to be found in nature.

- [ ] R. H. Macy & Company of New York City is the largest department store in the world.

- [ ] President James Monroe avoided all allusions to Biblical quotations in private letters and public utterances.

- [ ] In 1876, Professor Elias Loomis, of Western Reserve University, established the first scientific weather bureau in the United States.

- [ ] Antley Donald, famous pitcher for the New York Yankees, once threw a baseball at the rate of 94.7 miles per hour.

- [ ] The American robin is not a robin. It is a thrush.

- [ ] Thomas Jefferson is quoted more often and on more different subjects than any other president of the United States.

- [ ] A grasshopper is capable of jumping a distance of about two feet.

- [ ] It is as easy to swim in water ten feet deep as in water one hundred feet deep.

- [ ] The word *television* means "to see at a distance."

- [ ] Seventy-two muscles are used in speaking one word.

- [ ] The most prevalent infection in the world today is malaria.

- [ ] About 70 percent of hospital costs go to pay employees' salaries.

- [ ] The longest human beard ever recorded was eleven feet, six inches, grown by Hans N. Lanoseth in 1912.

- [ ] Silk was discovered about 2700 B.C.

- [ ] The windiest place on earth is in the Antarctic region.

- [ ] On August 1, 1873, San Francisco's famous cable streetcars were put into service.

- [ ] The oldest legislative body in the world was founded in Iceland, A.D. 930.

- [ ] Sixty-five pounds of cotton are used in the manufacture of an automobile.

- [ ] The Chicago electric elevated railroad, known as "the el," was opened for traffic June 2, 1883.

- [ ] There are eighteen calories in a teaspoon of sugar.

- [ ] The House committee to investigate un-American activities was formed May 26, 1938.

- [ ] Music plays no part in the typical religious service of orthodox Mohammedans.

- [ ] The last president of the United States to wear "knee breeches" was James Monroe.

- [ ] "D-Day" of World War II was June 6, 1944.

- [ ] A recent scientific survey shows that millions of Americans are both uncomfortable and unhappy with the names their parents have hung on them.

- [ ] The first motion picture "drive-in" theater was opened June 6, 1933.
- [ ] Assembly line production adopted by Henry Ford in his Detroit auto factory became effective on June 6, 1913.
- [ ] The three predominating colors in flowers are: white, red, and blue—in that order.
- [ ] There is no such thing as an irresistible force meeting an immovable object.
- [ ] A baby elephant sucks with its mouth, not with its trunk.
- [ ] The Japs attacked Pearl Harbor December 7, 1941.
- [ ] A "picture bride" is one whom the bridegroom has not seen before the marriage.
- [ ] The first telegraphic communication between New York City and Chicago was established June 10, 1848.
- [ ] There are at least fifteen hundred known varieties of mosquitoes.
- [ ] Grover Cleveland was a bachelor at the time he was elected president of the United States.
- [ ] There are 907 miles of railroad in the state of New Hampshire.
- [ ] On June 20, 1863, The National Bank of Davenport, Iowa, was the first to be chartered under the national banking law.
- [ ] The world-record attendance at a basketball game is seventy-five thousand—in Olympic Stadium, Berlin, Germany.
- [ ] During the Administration of President Woodrow Wilson, sheep were pastured on the White House lawn.
- [ ] On July 16, 1798, the first United States Marine Hospital was authorized by Congress.
- [ ] King George I, of England, was born in Germany and could not speak the language of the country he ruled.
- [ ] The thermometer was invented by a German inventor, Gabriel Fahrenheit. He died in 1736.
- [ ] In 1870, it took eight days to cross the United States by train.
- [ ] President Grover Cleveland once taught in a school for the blind.
- [ ] The inside of a refrigerator is cold because the heat has been pumped out of it.
- [ ] The greatest distance a baseball has ever been thrown was 426 feet, 9½ inches.
- [ ] The Confederate government was organized February 4, 1861, in Montgomery, Alabama.
- [ ] It is prophesied in the Bible that the Lord would shave with a razor. See Isaiah 7:20.
- [ ] Dry ice is solidified carbon dioxide.

- [ ] Spiders differ from insects in that they possess eight legs.

- [ ] There is no such thing as "martial law." So-called martial law is nothing but military control.

- [ ] The United States occupation forces organized the Berlin Airlift June 26, 1948.

- [ ] Color is a sensation and has no material existence.

- [ ] There was no known relationship between Noah and Daniel Webster.

- [ ] A bathometer is an instrument for indicating the depths of the sea beneath a moving vessel.

- [ ] The game of baseball was invented in 1839, by Abner Doubleday.

- [ ] In 1948, Alben W. Barkley, at the age of 71, became the oldest man ever to be elected vice president of the United States.

- [ ] The estimated weight of the Great Pyramid of Egypt is 6,648,000 tons.

- [ ] Four states in the United States are designated as common-wealths: Kentucky, Massachusetts, Pennsylvania, and Virginia.

- [ ] The Methodist Church was established May 24, 1738.

- [ ] Between seven and ten tons of sugar cane are required to produce a ton of sugar at the mill.

- [ ] The United States Constitution went into effect June 21, 1788.

- [ ] Campanology is the art or science of ringing bells.

- [ ] The cardinal virtues of the ancients were: justice, prudence, temperance, and fortitude.

- [ ] Cambric is the finest and thinnest of linen fabrics.

- [ ] George Washington became a Master Mason August 4, 1753.

- [ ] A collusion is a fradulent agreement whereby two or more parties seek to circumvent the law.

- [ ] Friends throw old shoes at newly wedded couples because it is considered a lucky omen.

- [ ] The country of Finland is smaller than the state of California.

- [ ] Except for fifty-five verses, all of the material found in Saint Mark is also found in Saint Matthew.

- [ ] Andrew Jackson was the first president of the United States to ride on a train, June 6, 1833.

- [ ] The English, not the Germans, invented the goose-step for its soldiers.

- [ ] Alcoholism is a ground for divorce in the majority of states.

- [ ] Only 3 percent of Norway is under cultivation.

- [ ] Ostriches do not bury their heads in the sand as many suppose.

- [ ] The United States has never issued a gold certificate below the denomination of ten dollars.
- [ ] Population-wise, Nevada is the smallest state in the United States.
- [ ] The dimensions of a regulation football field are: 360 feet long and 160 feet wide.
- [ ] The fairy hummingbird of Cuba is the smallest known bird in the world.
- [ ] Asia is four times as large as Europe.
- [ ] In 1935, the swastika became the national flag of Germany.
- [ ] A meter is 3.37 inches longer than a yard.
- [ ] The natural color of a goldfish is not gold.
- [ ] In 1874, Philadelphia became the first American city to have a zoo.
- [ ] The largest seed in the world is the double coconut, sometimes weighing forty pounds.
- [ ] Sprains occur in the ligaments; strains occur in the muscles.
- [ ] The Turkish people are the biggest consumers of cereal products.
- [ ] The first seeing eye dog was presented to a blind person on April 25, 1938.
- [ ] The average milk bottle is used thirty times before it breaks or is retired.
- [ ] La Paz, Bolivia, has the highest altitude of any city in the world.
- [ ] Ringworm is not a worm — it is a fungus.
- [ ] In the year of 1933, all school teachers in Germany were ordered to read Adolf Hitler's Mein Kampf.
- [ ] The longest mustache on record measured seventy-six inches.
- [ ] Approximately 75 percent of all ulcer patients are men.
- [ ] The League of Nations was established June 28, 1919, and dissolved in April of 1946.
- [ ] Mrs. Nellie Ross was the first woman director of the United States Mint.
- [ ] In England a spool of thread is called a "reel of cotton."
- [ ] Forty percent of the human body is normally composed of muscles.
- [ ] In 1626 Peter Minuit purchased Manhattan Island from the Indians for trinkets worth about twenty-four dollars.
- [ ] Camel's hair brushes are not made of camel's hair. They are made of squirrels' hair.
- [ ] It is possible for a good musician to tell whether a note is played on a Stradivarius or an ordinary violin.
- [ ] The average woman in the United States walks a distance of ten miles each day — one more than the average man.

- [ ] The famous "Little Jack Horner who sat in a corner" was a real boy.

- [ ] Sound does not travel in a vacuum.

- [ ] It is an established fact that married people live longer than those who remain single.

- [ ] Tattoo designs on the human body can be removed only by removing the skin itself.

- [ ] A wind with a speed of seventy-four miles or more is designated as a hurricane.

- [ ] The most accurate public clock in the world is in the window of the American Telephone and Telegraph building in New York City.

- [ ] Insulin was discovered in 1922 by Sir Frederick Banting and Dr. Charles Best.

- [ ] On April 12, 1938, the state of New York passed a law requiring medical tests for marriage license applicants, the first state to do so.

- [ ] A sheep is considered to be the most stupid creature in the world of zoology.

- [ ] The world's first train robbery took place on July 21, 1873, at Adair, Iowa, by the notorious outlaw Jesse James.

- [ ] The average depth of the ocean is about ten thousand feet.

- [ ] It takes 110,000 gallons of water to produce a ton of steel.

- [ ] Earliest wristwatches date from 1790.

- [ ] The first medical school in the United States was established in 1765, in Philadelphia, Pennsylvania.

- [ ] During World War II, it cost the United States $225,000 to kill an enemy soldier.

- [ ] President Grover Cleveland had an artificial jaw.

- [ ] Seven countries of the world have flags of red, white, and blue.

- [ ] The price of the pituitary gland of a pig is about forty dollars per pound.

- [ ] Twenty-four percent of the state of California is classified as desert.

- [ ] The Scots at first refused to cultivate potatoes because the Bible did not mention the plant.

- [ ] The average American family of today is comprised of 3.71 persons.

- [ ] On June 21, 1768, Dr. John Archer received the first Bachelor of Medicine degree to be conferred in the United States.

- [ ] The Soviet Union set up the "Berlin Blockade" June 24, 1948.

- [ ] Chinese typewriters are so complex that even a skilled operator cannot type at a rate of more than three or four words per minute.

- [ ] Birds cost the U.S. Air Force about $10 million a year in aircraft damage.

- [ ] Phi Beta Kappa was the first college fraternity in America.

- [ ] The average American's vacation trip is within two hundred miles of his home.

- [ ] The United States inaugurated Rural Free Delivery in 1896.

- [ ] Shrimp swim backwards, pushing themselves with their fan-shaped tails.

- [ ] The revolving door was invented August 7, 1888, by Theophilus Van Kannel, of Philadelphia, Pennsylvania.

- [ ] The late President John F. Kennedy established the world's record for being the fastest talker in public life. In a speech he made in December, 1961, he spoke at the rate of 327 words per minute.

- [ ] Colonel Daniel Huston Torrey was the author of the inscription on the Tomb of the Unknown Soldier in Arlington Cemetery.

- [ ] Iron that has been protected by a thin layer of zinc is called galvanized iron.

- [ ] Oxygen was discovered in 1774 by the English scientist Joseph Priestly.

- [ ] The original name of Columbia University was King's College.

- [ ] The Bureau of the Census was established as a permanent agency in 1902.

- [ ] The age of a tree can be determined by counting the concentric rings of its cross-section.

- [ ] Dr. John Mudd was the physician who treated John Wilkes Booth after he had assassinated Abraham Lincoln.

- [ ] The first motion picture in technicolor was shown June 4, 1929, in Rochester, New York, by George Eastman.

- [ ] In 1883, Susan Hayhurst became the first woman to graduate from a college of pharmacy.

- [ ] "Stars and Bars" was the name given the first Confederate flag.

- [ ] In the May, 1959, issue of the *Reader's Digest* there appeared the most expensive single advertisement to ever appear in a periodical. The 36-page insert cost the Ford Motor Company $877,000.

- [ ] More than three million Americans have hernias.

- [ ] The index finger of the Statue of Liberty measures eight feet in length.

- [ ] In 1873, E. Remington & Sons manufactured the first practical typewriter.

- [ ] The largest blue whale ever caught weighed 145 tons.

- [ ] There is a separate silk strand for each kernel on an ear of corn.

- [ ] John Milton used eight thousand different words in his poem, "Paradise Lost."

- [ ] The world's largest recorded hailstone weighed 1½ pounds, and was 17 inches in circumference. This hailstone fell in the little community of Potter, Nebraska, on July 6, 1928.

- [ ] Ten presidents of the United States were slaveholders at one time or another.

- [ ] A watermelon is 92 percent water.

- [ ] The whooping crane is the tallest bird in North America.

- [ ] An athlete runs faster outdoors than indoors.

- [ ] The "hot dog" probably originated at the Louisiana Purchase Exposition in Saint Louis, Missouri, in 1904.

- [ ] It never gets too cold to snow, but it often gets too cold to snow in flakes.

- [ ] The first revolving machine gun was invented by Richard Jordan Gatling, an American schoolteacher and physician, September 12, 1818.

- [ ] In 1813, the first delivery of mail by steamboat was authorized by Congress.

- [ ] Wine has been used in medical practice for more than two thousand years.

- [ ] On April 1, 1578, William Harvey, an English physician, discovered the circulation of blood.

- [ ] The library of Thomas Jefferson consisted of ten thousand volumes.

- [ ] North Dakota is the coldest state in the United States.

- [ ] At birth, the hippopotamus weighs about one hundred pounds.

- [ ] Frozen rain forms sleet, not snow.

- [ ] The first national vaccination legislation was enacted in 1813.

- [ ] In Amsterdam, Holland, more than one-third of the population owns bicycles.

- [ ] Schoolhouses were formerly painted red because red paint was the cheapest paint available.

- [ ] The capital of the state of Texas has been changed fifteen times.

- [ ] Cypress wood outlasts granite.

- [ ] Fish do not have a keen sense of hearing, but they do have a keen sense of smell.

- [ ] The United States National Banking System was created by statute on February 25, 1863.

- [ ] On March 10, 1903, H. C. Gammeter of Cleveland, Ohio, patented the first "duplicating machine."

- [ ] The age of a mountain sheep is determined by the number of rings on its horns.
- [ ] Lake Itasca in Minnesota is the birthplace of the mighty Mississippi River.
- [ ] The vocabulary of the average person consists of five to six thousand words.
- [ ] Snakes are immune to their own poison when it is swallowed.
- [ ] The accordion was invented in 1829, by Damian of Vienna.
- [ ] Charles A. Lindbergh made the first solo flight across the Atlantic Ocean on May 20-21, 1927.
- [ ] The linen bandages that were used to wrap Egyptian mummies averaged one thousand yards in length.
- [ ] John Knox of Scotland was the first man in all history to advocate compulsory education.
- [ ] The first national labor organization in the United States was called "Knights of Labor."
- [ ] In 1793, the southern states of the United States produced two-thirds of the world's cotton.
- [ ] The spot on which the sun shines first in the United States is Mount Katahdin in the state of Maine.
- [ ] Hydrogen is the most common element in the universe.
- [ ] The bat is extemely sensitive to touch.
- [ ] Martin Van Buren was the first president of the United States elected as a "dark horse."
- [ ] The barometer was invented by Evangelista Torricelli, in 1643.
- [ ] On April 17, 1903, Henry Ford gave his first automobile an initial road test.
- [ ] The first power-producing public utility was built in New York City in 1882.
- [ ] More than twenty-six hundred buildings were destroyed by fire in downtown Baltimore, Maryland, in 1904.
- [ ] The country of Egypt has the lowest suicide rate in the world.
- [ ] On May 15, 1930, Miss Ellen Church became the first airline hostess.
- [ ] The world's largest spider measured 3 ½ inches in body length.
- [ ] There are more than one thousand types of cancer.
- [ ] Dogs are now being insured against accidents, sickness, and disease.
- [ ] A skilled Eskimo and his wife can build an igloo in less than an hour.
- [ ] The ancient Romans used beans for voting — white beans were affirmative votes; dark beans negative ones.

- [ ] General McKay invented the bayonet in 1689.
- [ ] On October 3, 1863, President Abraham Lincoln issued a proclamation designating the last Thursday in November as Thanksgiving Day.
- [ ] An ordinary white oak tree may give off as much as 150 gallons of moisture through its leaves in a single summer day.
- [ ] Generals Robert E. Lee and Ulysses S. Grant fought on the same side in the war with Mexico in 1848.
- [ ] The world's record alimony payment is $11,550,000.
- [ ] Vatican City comprises an area of 108.7 acres.
- [ ] A flea is capable of moving a weight hundreds of times heavier than himself.
- [ ] In 1948, Dr. Leslie Swigart Kent of Eugene, Oregon, became the first woman to be elected president of a State Medical Society.
- [ ] Eagles occupy one dwelling place generation after generation.
- [ ] Adult king cobra snakes commonly measure fifteen feet or more.
- [ ] The Bible forbids tattooing. See Leviticus 19:28.
- [ ] On September 18, 1793, President George Washington laid the cornerstone of the Capitol Building of the United States in Washington, D.C.
- [ ] In 1923, Thomas Buck Hine invented the first smoke screen for concealing the movement of troops and ships.
- [ ] Women in the United States spend about seven billion dollars a year on drug-store and beauty-shop skin treatments.
- [ ] A rain of fish occurred in 1817 at Appin, in Scotland.
- [ ] Twelve pounds of nitrogen per acre falls on the earth each year as a result of lightning.
- [ ] On March 26, 1943, Elsie S. Ott, an army nurse, became the first woman to receive an air medal.
- [ ] On January 1, 1863, President Abraham Lincoln signed the Emancipation Proclamation freeing the slaves.
- [ ] Lie-detecting devices are from 75 to 85 percent accurate.
- [ ] The Tomb of the Unknown Soldier of the American Revolution is in the churchyard of the old Presbyterian meeting house in Alexandria, Virginia.
- [ ] Belgium has the highest per capita beer consumption, with 34.3 gallons per annum.
- [ ] The penny postal card was placed on sale for the first time by the United States Post Office on May 1, 1873.
- [ ] Kharkov Prison in Russia is the largest prison in the world, and has, at times, accommodated forty thousand inmates.

- [ ] Martin Van Buren was the first professional politician to become president of the United States.
- [ ] The peanut is a fruit, not a true nut.
- [ ] In 1900 the average bride and groom could expect thirty years of marriage; today's newlyweds can expect forty-three years of life together.
- [ ] More than 90 percent of flowers have either an unpleasant odor or none at all.
- [ ] It is possible to hear corn grow.
- [ ] Some species of bamboo, a giant perennial grass, bloom only once every 120 years.
- [ ] The geographic center of North America is about fifty miles west of Devil's Lake in North Dakota.
- [ ] Harry S. Truman was the first president in the history of the United States to receive an annual salary of $100,000.
- [ ] The first bathtub installed in the United States was installed in a Cincinnati, Ohio, home in 1842. It was made of mahogany and was lined with sheet metal.
- [ ] One out of every ten trucks we meet on our highways today carry explosives, flamables, or poisons.
- [ ] If the hair on a normal head were shorn and woven into rope, it could support a weight of ten tons.
- [ ] The pronghorn antelope is found only in North America and has no close relatives.
- [ ] On May 6, 1833, the first steel plow was made by John Deere, a blacksmith in Grand Detour, Illinois.
- [ ] The greatest number of eclipses possible in one year is seven.
- [ ] Women were first sworn into the United States Navy on July 7, 1948.
- [ ] Benjamin Franklin taught himself three foreign languages.
- [ ] There are a total of 485 active volcanoes in the world.
- [ ] The word *communist* was first coined in the secret revolutionary societies of Paris, France, in the 1830s.
- [ ] Eighteen miles per hour is the highest measured speed for a reptile on land.
- [ ] Robert Earl Hughes of Fish Hook, Illinois, weighed 378 pounds when he was ten years old.
- [ ] The Republic of Israel was established April 23, 1948.
- [ ] In 1723, Dr. Daniel Turner became the first physician to receive an honorary medical degree.
- [ ] Damascus is the oldest city in the world.

- [ ] The granddaughter of Thomas Jefferson was the first child **born in** the White House — in 1806.

- [ ] "Jasmine" by Tuvache of Egypt is the most costly perfume in the world. It now retails in America for ninety dollars per ounce.

- [ ] On April 18, 1953, in Griffith Stadium, Mickey Mantle hit a home run that traveled about 565 feet.

- [ ] Only three presidents of the United States were millionaires when elected to office: Franklin D. Rooosevelt, Theodore Roosevelt, and Herbert Hoover.

- [ ] The largest English-speaking city south of Miami, Florida, is Kingston, Jamaica.

- [ ] Five hundred thousand gallons of water are used to launch a single intercontinental missile.

- [ ] The venom of a female black widow spider is more potent than that of a rattlesnake.

- [ ] Jacqueline Cochran was the first woman to fly faster than the speed of sound.

- [ ] The game of volleyball was invented in 1895, by William G. Morgan.

- [ ] On May 11, 1928, Station WGY, Schenectady, New York, began the first regularly scheduled television programs.

- [ ] At 4,145 miles, the Nile River is the longest river in the world.

- [ ] Airmail stamps were first issued May 13, 1918.

- [ ] In 1862, Abraham Lincoln instituted the first income tax law in American history.

- [ ] John Keats and Robert Louis Stevenson wrote their greatest books while weakened by tuberculosis.

- [ ] Sea water and healthy human blood have almost identical constituencies.

- [ ] The oldest encyclopedia which is still in existence was compiled in the first century A.D. by a Roman writer by the name of Pliny.

- [ ] Honey contains all the vitamins which nutritionists consider necessary to health.

- [ ] The first federal workmen's compensation law was approved by Congress on May 30, 1908.

- [ ] Postum was first manufactured in the barn of Charles W. Post.

- [ ] On June 9, 1943, Congress passed an act providing for "pay-as-you-go" income tax deduction.

- [ ] The capsicum hot pepper is the hottest of all spices.

- [ ] Wines and beer are the most acid of all alcoholic beverages.

- [ ] Water is about eight hundred times the weight of the atmosphere.

- [ ] Alfred Tennyson was eighty-three years old when he wrote "Crossing the Bar."
- [ ] On May 20, 1918, the warship *New Mexico* became the first warship to be propelled by electricity.
- [ ] George Washington, according to his account books, paid from ten to fifteen cents each for pins.
- [ ] The nine most useful English words are: *and, be, it, of, the, will, I, have,* and *you.*
- [ ] Eighteen percent of Vermont's population is over fifty-five years of age.
- [ ] The burning of one cigarette produces approximately two milligrams of nicotine.
- [ ] The lowest spot in Death Valley, California, is 279.1 feet below sea level.
- [ ] An object that weighs five pounds on the earth would weigh two pounds on the planet Mercury.
- [ ] On December 27, 1932, Radio City Music Hall, the largest indoor theater in the world, was opened to the public in New York City.
- [ ] A "curtain lecture" is a private scolding received by a husband from his wife.
- [ ] Maine is the only state in the United States that adjoins only one other state.
- [ ] The first professional football game was played in 1895, in Latrobe, Pennsylvania.
- [ ] Henry Ford first introduced his famous Model T Ford October 1, 1908.
- [ ] At least 50 percent of the Negroes in America belong to the Baptist Church.
- [ ] Steam is water that is expanded sixteen hundred times its original volume.
- [ ] When a key on the piano is struck, the result is a tone, not a note.
- [ ] The longest navigable inland waterway in the world is the Amazon River. Seagoing vessels can ascend it for a distance of twenty-three hundred miles.
- [ ] Nitrogen is the basic ingredient of practically every explosive used in warfare.
- [ ] It is impossible for gasoline to burn without oxygen.
- [ ] The United States Government Printing Office was founded in March, 1861.
- [ ] Florida has the longest shoreline of any state in the conterminous United States.
- [ ] Not all common members of the deer family have gallbladders.

- [ ] The president of the United States should be addressed as "Mr. President" or "sir."
- [ ] Gold in its pure form is not often used for jewelry or coinage.
- [ ] On June 8, 1869, Ives W. McGaffey of Chicago, Illinios, gave us the vacuum cleaner.
- [ ] The largest sum of money ever paid in a breach of promise suit was $140,000.
- [ ] More than one out of five people in the United States play some kind of musical instrument.
- [ ] Chewing gum was invented by William F. Semple of Mount Vernon, Ohio, on December 28, 1869.
- [ ] The country of Iceland has the highest consumption of protein per capita.
- [ ] Charles Darwin's *The Origin of Species* was published November 24, 1859.
- [ ] Balboa discovered the Pacific Ocean September 25, 1513.
- [ ] Three-fourths of all sulphur consumed in the United States goes into the manufacture of sulphuric acid.
- [ ] The first postal savings bank in America was opened in 1911.
- [ ] Flogging was abolished as punishment in the United States Army on August 5, 1861.
- [ ] John Pussey invented the book match in 1892.
- [ ] The first tank to be used in battle was "Little Willie," which saw service in the Battle of Flors in France on September 15, 1916.
- [ ] It is possible for the common housefly to bite.
- [ ] Andrew Jackson was the only president of the United States to fight a duel.
- [ ] On March 7, 1908, the mayor of Cincinnati, Ohio, told the city council that no woman was physically fit to operate an automobile.
- [ ] The first photograph was taken in 1826.
- [ ] Ducks do not get wet because their feathers are kept in an oily condition by small oil glands.
- [ ] "Power politics" is international politics played by nations instead of by parties and individuals.
- [ ] The biggest bicycle factory in the world is located in Nottingham, England.
- [ ] James Whitcomb Riley, the Hoosier poet, was born October 7, 1849. On this same day, Edgar Allen Poe died.
- [ ] Honey helps to promote sound and refreshing sleep because it is a body sedative.
- [ ] A female mackerel lays about 500,000 eggs at a time.

- [ ] Horses breathe only through their nostrils.
- [ ] Charles O'Connor, a noted New York lawyer, was the first Roman Catholic to be nominated for the presidency of the United States.
- [ ] The most intense rainfall ever recorded was 1.23 inches in one minute, at Unionville, Maryland, July 4, 1956.
- [ ] Jefferson Davis was elected president of the Confederacy on February 9, 1870.
- [ ] On February 11, 1808, anthracite coal was burned as a fuel for the first time in the United States by Judge Jesse Fell in his home at Wilkes-Barre, Pennsylvania.
- [ ] The age of the oldest snake on record was twenty-nine years, forty-two days.
- [ ] Two presidents of the United States, Andrew Jackson and Rutherford B. Hayes, were born posthumously (after their fathers had died).
- [ ] Harriet Beecher Stowe's famous book, *Uncle Tom's Cabin,* was published March 20, 1852. It was the first American novel to sell one million copies.
- [ ] The system of placing tax stamps on cigarette packages was inaugurated July 20, 1868.
- [ ] Walter Hunt of New York City startled the world by patenting the safety pin—on April 10, 1849.
- [ ] Any plum which has sufficient sugar in its substance to dry without souring is called a prune.
- [ ] The largest bullfighting ring in the world is located in Mexico City. It has a seating capacity of forty-eight thousand.
- [ ] To protect their eardrums, gunmen open their mouths while firing large guns.
- [ ] "America" or "My Country, 'Tis of Thee," was first sung in public by Boston schoolchildren on July 4, 1832.
- [ ] There are no tigers in Africa.
- [ ] Forty-one percent of the moon is not visible from the earth at any time.
- [ ] On September 1, 1878, Emma Nutt became the first woman telephone operator.
- [ ] The turbot fish lays approximately fourteen million eggs during its lifetime.
- [ ] A normally healthy person can lose as much as one-third of his blood without fatal results.
- [ ] Mother-in-law Day was first celebrated on March 5, 1934, in Amarillo, Texas.
- [ ] In the field of politics, a political "boss" is one who controls his party in a city, district, or state.

- [ ] It is customary for the government to pay the funeral expenses of presidents who die in office.
- [ ] The first piano ever built was built in Florence, Italy, about 1720.
- [ ] Of a steel ship and a wooden ship of the same dimensions, the steel ship is lighter in weight.
- [ ] The highest ransom ever extracted in a kidnaping case, $600,000, was paid in September 1953.
- [ ] On June 11, 1939, the king and queen of England tasted their first hot dogs at a picnic given by President and Mrs. Franklin D. Roosevelt at Hyde Park, New York.
- [ ] Roquefort cheese was accidentally discovered by an anonymous shepherd on June 4, 1070.
- [ ] The highest number of which a human mind can conceive is a centillion.
- [ ] It was on September 22, 1692, that the last person in the American colonies was hanged for witchcraft.
- [ ] *Fortnight* is a contraction of "fourteen nights." It has been supplanted by "two weeks" in the United States.
- [ ] The human heart pumps 4,320 gallons of blood every day.
- [ ] Washing eggs will cause them to spoil quicker.
- [ ] Eighty-four percent of a raw apple is water.
- [ ] The oldest tennis court in the world is located in Paris, France. It was built in 1496.
- [ ] Oklahoma, Arizona, and New Mexico contain nearly half the entire Indian population of the United States.
- [ ] On October 24, 1901, Mrs. Anna Edson Taylor, a schoolteacher, became the first woman to go over Niagara Falls in a barrel, thus fulfilling a lifetime ambition.
- [ ] The first football "bowl" game was played in January 1902, in Pasadena, California.
- [ ] It is possible to see a rainbow as a complete circle.
- [ ] The Distinguished Service Cross and the Distinguished Service Medal were authorized by Congress, July 9, 1918.
- [ ] Levulose, found in honey, is the sweetest of all common sugars.
- [ ] Custer's last stand took place on June 25, 1876, at the battle of Little Big Horn, in Montana.
- [ ] The largest iceberg on record covered twelve thousand square miles; it was 208 miles long and 60 miles broad. It was first sighted November 12, 1956.
- [ ] The largest cake ever baked weighed twenty-five thousand pounds. It was made in August, 1962, in Seattle, Washington. The cake was twenty-five feet high, with a circumference of sixty feet.

- [ ] It is in keeping with flag etiquette to wash or dry clean an American flag.

- [ ] Virginia Dare was born August 18, 1587, "the first child born of English parents on American soil."

- [ ] The United States Medical Corps was organized April 14, 1818.

- [ ] The highest waterfall in the world, Angel Falls in Venezuela, has a total drop of 3,121 feet.

- [ ] Earmuffs were patented by Chester Greenwood of Farmington, Maine, on March 13, 1887.

- [ ] Barre, Vermont is the largest granite-cutting center in the world.

- [ ] The greatest number of operations ever performed on one patient was 410.

- [ ] President George Washington once said "I would rather be in my grave than in the presidency."

- [ ] The largest living thing on earth is the General Sherman Tree in California. It is 272 feet, 4 inches tall.

- [ ] On December 19, 1732, Benjamin Franklin began publication of *Poor Richard's Almanac*.

- [ ] A rabbit produced by artificial impregnation was exhibited to the New York Academy of Medicine, November 1, 1939.

- [ ] More than 15 percent of married couples never bear children.

- [ ] Daylight saving time was introduced in the United States on March 31, 1918.

- [ ] The United States Marines were made a permanent organization July 11, 1798.

- [ ] One cup of rice becomes three cups when cooked.

- [ ] Adhesive postage stamps were introduced February 15, 1842, in New York City.

- [ ] The highest price ever paid for an orchid, $3,234, was paid by Mrs. H. F. C. Sander of London, England, in 1906.

- [ ] A piece of pie eaten just once each week will add more than three pounds of body weight in a year.

- [ ] Dr. Truman J. Martin, a physician of Buffalo, New York, became the first holder of an automobile insurance policy, February 1, 1898.

- [ ] Giant tortoises have a greater life span than man does.

- [ ] Pigeons are especially noted for their uncanny instinct for finding their way home.

- [ ] The first pure food law was enacted in the United States June 26, 1848.

- [ ] Airplane passenger service was inaugurated May 3, 1919, when a pilot flew two women from New York City to Atlantic City, New Jersey.

- [ ] Alexander Graham Bell was called a fool when he exhibited his telephone at the Centennial Exposition in Philadelphia.

- [ ] The largest stained glass window in the world measures three hundred feet in length and is twenty-three feet high. It is in Idlewild International Airport, New York City.

- [ ] Children sometimes eat dirt in search of the potassium which is very necessary for their body growth.

- [ ] The Public Works Administration became effective on July 8, 1933.

- [ ] William McKinley, in 1889, was the first president of the United States to ride in an automobile.

- [ ] The first transatlantic cable was completed August 5, 1858.

- [ ] A "bread and butter letter" is the popular name given to a brief note of thanks written by a departed guest to his host or hostess.

- [ ] After trying for twenty-three years, Commander Robert E. Peary reached the North Pole on April 6, 1900.

- [ ] The weight of the largest book in the world was five hundred pounds. It was published in Baltimore, Maryland, in 1925.

- [ ] "Dyed in the wool" is applied to any uncompromising partisan, particularly a conservative "of the deepest dye."

- [ ] The horse can sleep either standing up or lying down.

- [ ] Belfast, Ireland, is the largest linen manufacturing center in the world.

- [ ] Fingerprinting in federal penitentiaries began November 2, 1904, in the United States penitentiary at Leavenworth, Kansas.

- [ ] A naturalized citizen of the United States cannot be legally deported to the country of his birth, or to any other country.

- [ ] There are seventy-two well-known wine types on the American market today.

- [ ] The longest hunger strike on record lasted ninety-four days, in the year 1920.

- [ ] Corn whiskey is made of grain mash, two-fifths of which is corn.

- [ ] On October 6, 1863, a Turkish bath, the first in America, opened in Brooklyn, New York.

- [ ] In Hawaii, the word *aloha* means both "hello" and "goodbye" and this causes no end of confusion.

- [ ] The largest check in the history of banking was in the amount of $334,867,807.68 and was drawn by Lazard Brothers, Ltd. on January 24, 1961.

- [ ] The coffee percolator was displayed to an eager world by James Nason, of Franklin, Massachusetts, on December 26, 1865.

- [ ] Forty to fifty tons of ore must be refined to obtain one ton of uranium.

- [ ] Twenty years have been added to the average life expectancy in America since 1900.

- [ ] One gram of carbohydrates will yield four calories of energy.

- [ ] Sir Walter Raleigh was executed in London on October 29, 1618.

- [ ] The Eastman Kodak was first marketed April 24, 1888.

- [ ] A woman can talk with less effort than a man because her vocal cords are shorter than those of the male. Not only does this cause her voice to be higher pitched, it also requires less air to agitate the cords making it possible for her to talk more, yet expend less energy.

- [ ] The city of New Orleans, Louisiana, was founded August 25, 1718, and named in honor of the Duke of Orleans of France.

- [ ] On May 2, 1865, President Andrew Johnson offered a reward of $100,000 for the capture of Jefferson Davis, president of the Confederacy.

- [ ] William Henry Harrison was the oldest man every to be elected to the presidency of the United States. He was sixty-eight.

- [ ] There are forty-seven different kinds of headaches.

- [ ] A thermometer registers colder if it has first been thrust into hot water.

- [ ] Key West, Florida, is closer to Cuba than to the mainland of the United States.

- [ ] On May 15, 1933, the first voice amplification system was installed in the United States Senate.

- [ ] Psalm 118:8 is the middle verse of the Bible.

- [ ] Three percent of the children born in America are mentally retarded.

- [ ] John Tyler was the first president of the United States to be photographed while in office.

- [ ] In all the world of nature, a fish is the most difficult living thing for man to train to obey him.

- [ ] On January 7, 1914, the Panama Canal was successfully navigated, inaugurating a new era.

- [ ] It is not mandatory that the national flag be flown from sunrise to sunset.

- [ ] Leaf lard is made from the fat surrounding the kidneys of swine.

- [ ] Adult moths do no damage to clothing because they do not eat anything.

- [ ] The highest temperature ever recorded in the United States was 134 degrees. This occurred in Death Valley, California, on July 10, 1913.

- [ ] Paul Revere made his famous ride on April 18, 1775.

- [ ] The push-key adding machine was patented on February 5, 1850.

- [ ] Charles Graham, of New York City, is revered by dentists for having come up with some workable, if primitive, artificial teeth on March 9, 1822.

- [ ] New Hampshire was the only colony of the original thirteen which was not invaded by the enemy during the American Revolution.

- [ ] The iron lung was first used October 12, 1918, at Children's Hospital, Boston, Massachusetts, on a little girl suffering from infantile paralysis.

- [ ] Canada has two official languages: English and French.

- [ ] Children of midgets are usually of normal size.

- [ ] Railroad ties are laid approximately twenty-one inches apart, measuring from center to center.

- [ ] A new-born kangaroo is about one inch in length.

- [ ] Irish stew did not originate in Ireland. In fact, it is unknown in Ireland.

- [ ] The longest recorded flight ever made by a pigeon was fifty-four hundred miles. It was made in fifty-five days in 1854.

- [ ] There are about five thousand languages in the world.

- [ ] Trained seals used in circuses are not true seals, they are sea lions. Fur seals cannot live in captivity.

- [ ] Socrates, the Greek philosopher, left no writings of his own. His philosophy is known only through writings of his pupil, Plato.

- [ ] The cost of manufacturing the first atomic bomb was two billion dollars.

- [ ] There are twenty-eight states in Mexico plus a federal capital district.

- [ ] About three hours are required for a frozen sandwich to thaw at room temperature.

- [ ] The most expensive land in the world is in the city of London, England.

- [ ] The Packard was the first automobile to cross the American continent under its own power. The trip, in 1903, required fifty-two days.

- [ ] A competent newspaper man writes an average of about one thousand words per hour.

- [ ] Apple cider vinegar is an excellent antiseptic.

- [ ] Australia is the largest wool-producing country in the world.

- [ ] Grape juice will quench thirst promptly, even when taken in small amounts.

- [ ] The highest man-made rotary speed ever achieved is ninety million revolutions per minute.

- [ ] It is almost impossible to find a seafaring man who is an atheist.
- [ ] The first roll-film camera was patented by George Eastman September 4, 1888.
- [ ] Iodine is the most healing agent found in the ocean.
- [ ] William Howard Taft was the largest president of the United States. He weighed 280 pounds.
- [ ] The common housefly is probably the most dangerous insect in America. It spreads at least twenty dangerous diseases.
- [ ] Arizona, with an average rainfall of only 7.81 inches annually, is the driest state in the United States.
- [ ] A wild tiger is easier to train than one born in captivity.
- [ ] The Pilgrim Fathers sailed from Plymouth, England, September 6, 1620.
- [ ] Thomas Jefferson was the founder of the University of Virginia.
- [ ] Fingernails grow faster than toenails.
- [ ] The weight of the average cigarette is one gram.
- [ ] There are thirty-four miles of railroad in the District of Columbia.
- [ ] Helium weighs about one-seventh as much as air.
- [ ] The women of the United States buy forty million girdles each year.
- [ ] Italics are 2.7 percent more difficult to read than Roman type.
- [ ] Ducks and geese can fly at a speed of seventy miles per hour in level flight.
- [ ] Sight is the strongest of human senses.
- [ ] There is a point directly behind the jet engine's exhaust where no sound whatever is registered.
- [ ] The mental development of a moron does not exceed that of a normal twelve-year-old boy.
- [ ] President William McKinley served thirty years as superintendent of a Methodist Sunday school.
- [ ] A mouse finds it difficult to distinguish between two baseballs at a distance of three feet.
- [ ] The greatest depth of the ocean yet found is 6.7 miles.
- [ ] If one quart of water and one quart of alcohol were mixed, the resulting mixture would be slightly less than two quarts.
- [ ] The blood of a human being makes a complete circuit of the body every twenty-three seconds.
- [ ] At a depth of fifty feet, rocks remain at the same temperature throughout the year.
- [ ] Thomas Jefferson could read the Bible in four languages: Greek, Latin, French, and English.

- [ ] There are fifty joints in each leg of a daddy longlegs.
- [ ] The word *sermon* is not in the Bible.
- [ ] The capacity of the human stomach is about two quarts.
- [ ] If a cow inhales garlic, she will impart that garlic flavor to her milk.
- [ ] The Dominion of Canada has a greater land area than the continental United States.
- [ ] In the fifth century A.D. the barbers in Rome extracted teeth, treated wounds, and bled patients as a part of their professional work.
- [ ] The Anti-Saloon League was organized in 1894.
- [ ] Sick horses don't kick people.
- [ ] In Africa, the seed of the date palm is often roasted and used as coffee.
- [ ] The average American makes 382 phone calls each year.
- [ ] Sheep have three times as many red corpuscles as human beings do.
- [ ] The name of Portland, Oregon, was decided upon by flipping a coin.
- [ ] Abraham Lincoln was the tallest president of the United States. He was six feet, four inches tall.
- [ ] Frogs and toads are often confused. In general, frogs have smooth skins and toads have warty skins.
- [ ] Dice were invented in 1244, B.C.
- [ ] The word *textile* is applied to any woven material.
- [ ] There are more than one hundred different breeds of domesticated dogs.
- [ ] The words *republic* and *democracy* do not occur in the Declaration of Independence.
- [ ] Rattlesnakes do not lay eggs. They give birth to their living young.
- [ ] Studies recently conducted by a group of sociologists show that a divorced woman is an appreciably better marriage risk than a divorced man.
- [ ] The book of Esther (in the Bible) does not contain the name of God.
- [ ] President Calvin Coolidge was an inveterate smoker of cigars.
- [ ] The eggs of the water flea will hatch ten years after they are laid.
- [ ] A person is said to be "up to snuff" when he is worldly wise, well informed, and not easily deceived.
- [ ] Petroleum was first discovered August 27, 1859.
- [ ] The three most level states in the United States are: Louisiana, Delaware, and Illinois.

- [ ] A man could jump over the Washington Monument if he could jump as high in proportion to his size as a flea can.

- [ ] The Amazon River flows upstream along its banks at certain points where tributaries join the river.

- [ ] A woman is not legally obligated to assume her husband's name when she marries him.

- [ ] About 35 percent of the earth's surface never receives any snow-fall.

- [ ] Napoleon died in exile on the Island of St. Helena in 1821.

- [ ] Male polar bears do not hibernate; instead, they roam through the long winter nights.

- [ ] The national flower of the United States is the goldenrod.

- [ ] A temperature of about 125 degrees below zero is required to freeze alcohol.

- [ ] On February 13, 1741, Andrew Bradford of Philadelphia, Pennsylvania, published the first magazine in America.

- [ ] It is possible to shatter a diamond with an ordinary hammer by hitting it at the proper cleavage with great force.

- [ ] There is a spot in the United States where a house could be built with each of its four corners in a different state. That spot is at the common meeting point of Utah, Colorado, Arizona, and New Mexico.

- [ ] Phillips Brooks was the greatest preacher the Episcopal Church has produced in America.

- [ ] So far as is known, President Andrew Johnson never went to school a day in his life.

- [ ] The highest point of the earth, with an elevation of 29,141 feet, is the top of Mount Everest in southern Tibet.

- [ ] At least three persons must be involved in a disturbance for it to rate being called a "riot."

- [ ] Volcano ash has been known to remain hot for a period of nearly one hundred years.

- [ ] The largest United States flag ever constructed was 270 feet long and 90 feet wide.

- [ ] Congress has granted "franking privilege" to widows of presidents.

- [ ] Jockeys ride with short stirrups so that weight may be placed on the horse's withers instead of his back.

- [ ] There are four ways of catching fish: nets, baited hooks, traps, and spears.

- [ ] The motto of the United States Post Office is: Certainty, Security, and Celerity.

- [ ] Eli Whitney received a patent for his cotton gin on March 14, 1794.

- [ ] About one person out of a million are injured or killed by lightning throughout the world each year.

- [ ] The wife of President Millard Fillmore selected the first books for a permanent library in the White House.

- [ ] On January 4, 1885, Mary Gartside, age twenty-two, of Davenport, Iowa, became the first person in the United States to have her appendix removed.

- [ ] A polygon is a many-sided figure.

- [ ] The Mayflower Pilgrims did not all go ashore the same day. The women first went ashore November 24, 1620, thirteen days after the men.

- [ ] One thing was peculiar about the presidency of Jefferson Davis (of the Confederate States of America). He was preceded by no one in office and had no successor.

- [ ] Two birds, the cuckoo of Europe and the cowbird of America, do not rear their young.

- [ ] There are twenty "baby teeth."

- [ ] In 1670, William Penn was fined for not removing his hat in court. He was imprisoned for refusing to pay the fine.

- [ ] Andrew Jackson was the only president of the United States whose parents were born abroad.

- [ ] The average weight of a man's brain is forty-nine ounces; that of the average female, forty-four ounces.

- [ ] Thomas A. Edison did not make the first electric light bulb as is popularly believed.

- [ ] It is unlawful to send by mail a card "dunning" the person to whom it is addressed for a debt or an account past due.

- [ ] Of all the presidents of the United States, James Madison was the smallest in stature. He weighed less than a hundred pounds, and was under five feet, four inches in height.

- [ ] The Merchandise Mart Building in Chicago, Illinois, covers two blocks; it has four million square feet of floor.

- [ ] Snow is composed of about nine-tenths air and only one-tenth water.

- [ ] The right bank of a river is the bank to the right of a person looking downstream.

- [ ] "Boogie Woogie music" originated in the lumber and turpentine camps of Texas and Louisiana.

- [ ] Hairs on the human head do not grow from the ends, as many people seem to think. They grow only from the roots.

- [ ] The watermelon is believed to be a native of tropical Africa.

- [ ] The longest sentence ever written contained 823 words, 93 commas, 51 semicolons, and 4 dashes.

- [ ] It is legal for private individuals and business firms to sell postage stamps at a profit or loss if they desire to do so.

- [ ] Coal was first discovered in the United States in 1673 by two French explorers, Joliet and Marquette.

- [ ] The male seal refuses to eat during the mating season, from spring until August.

- [ ] Diamond is ninety times as hard as the next hardest mineral, corundum.

- [ ] Three presidents of the United States were married during their term of office: John Tyler, Grover Cleveland, and Woodrow Wilson.

- [ ] Abraham Lincoln never used tobacco in any form.

- [ ] The first nudist organization in America was the American League for Physical Culture, established in New York City on December 5, 1929.

- [ ] People like to sing in the bathtub because they can hear themselves easily in a small, highly reverberant room.

- [ ] Jesus Christ spoke the Aramaic language, a dialect of Galilee.

- [ ] The Greek philosopher, Thales, in 585 B.C. accurately predicted an eclipse of the sun.

- [ ] A tomato plant takes thirty gallons of water from the soil during its growing period.

- [ ] Instead of expanding, mercury contracts when it freezes.

- [ ] The heart of a normal man will beat thirty-eight million times each year.

- [ ] Trees and plants receive about 90 percent of their nutrition from the atmosphere and only 10 percent from the soil.

- [ ] The backbone of a camel is as straight as the backbone of a horse.

- [ ] Idaho is the only state in the United States over which no foreign flag has ever flown.

- [ ] President Andrew Jackson did not object to being seen in public smoking a pipe or chewing tobacco.

- [ ] In Paris, France, on July 6, 1885, Louis Pasteur inoculated the first human being, a boy who had been bitten by a dog.

- [ ] All the instruments in an orchestra are tuned to the note of middle A.

- [ ] The Sahara comprises 3,500,000 square miles.

- [ ] An ordinary drinking glass holds about fifty teaspoonsful.

- [ ] Cherrapunji, India, is the wettest place on earth, with an average annual rainfall of 427 inches.

- [ ] Arabic numerals were first used in India, not in Arabia.

- [ ] Of all the animals tested so far, only the monkeys and apes seem capable of color perception.

- [ ] The ancient Egyptians first began to make glass 3500 B. C.

- [ ] A Japanese cook devotes as much time and attention to arrangement and color scheme of foods as she does to taste.

- [ ] Twenty-twenty vision simply means that a person can see what he should see at a distance of twenty feet.

- [ ] When the sight of one eye is lost, one's vision is reduced by about one-fifth.

- [ ] The first bridge composed entirely of iron was built in 1776, in England.

- [ ] More than 75 percent of the more common types of birthmarks occur on the face.

- [ ] There are 132 rooms in the White House.

- [ ] World War II was never officially ended by the United States.

- [ ] Hail never occurs when the surface temperature is below freezing.

- [ ] The American Association for the Advancement of Atheism was incorporated in New York State on November 16, 1925.

- [ ] In journalism, the famous 5-W formula is: Who, What, When, Where, and Why.

- [ ] There are eight sinuses in the head of human beings.

- [ ] Castor oil is considered a specific remedy for soft corns.

- [ ] A planetarium is a mechanical device which makes the planetary system intelligible to an audience.

- [ ] William Shakespeare, the celebrated poet, died in 1616, at the age of fifty-two.

- [ ] The blue jay is a vegetarian except in the summer.

- [ ] In the vicinity of East Cape, Florida, lies the southernmost point of land in the continental United States.

- [ ] The nation's first gas well was drilled in 1821, at Fredonia, New York.

- [ ] Franklin D. Roosevelt traveled 243,827 miles by train during his terms as president of the United States.

- [ ] None of the people on board the Mayflower, when it sailed for the New World in 1620, had a middle name.

- [ ] In the womb, the heart of a female child usually beats faster than that of a male child.

- [ ] The Bible explains how butter is made. See Proverbs 30:33.

- [ ] The wife of President Andrew Jackson, who died before her husband was inaugurated, was buried in the satin dress she had planned to wear on that occasion.

- [ ] Benjamin Franklin became a printer because his father couldn't afford to give him a formal education.

- [ ] People who are covered by surgical insurance undergo about twice as many operations as people who are not covered.

- [ ] James Madison was defeated for reelection to the legislature in 1777 because he refused to provide the voters with free whiskey.

- [ ] The first commercial creamery in the United States was established in 1856, in Orange County, New York.

- [ ] A state of intoxication is a condition in which there is recognizable disturbance of intellect, movement, and coordination.

- [ ] *One* appears sixteen times on the face and back of the one-dollar bill.

- [ ] A boy could jump over his father's barn if his jumping ability was proportionate to that of a grasshopper.

- [ ] In 1883, the first official telephone booth was patented.

- [ ] George Whitefield, a Methodist minister, originated the modern revival meeting.

- [ ] The total calorie content of a typical American daily diet is about twenty-eight hundred calories.

- [ ] Normally in the Supreme Court of the United States, each side is allowed one hour in which to present its case.

- [ ] A notch in a tree will remain the same distance from the ground as the tree grows.

- [ ] The Bible commands Christians to kiss one another. See Romans 16:16.

- [ ] James K. Polk was the only president of the United States to have been Speaker of the House of Representatives.

- [ ] The wheel is one of the greatest inventions of all time.

- [ ] In 1790, the United States issued the first patent.

- [ ] Eight miles of the Seine River is in the city of Paris, France.

- [ ] The second safest place to work in the entire industrial world is in an ammunition plant.

- [ ] Memorial Day was first celebrated in 1868.

- [ ] The ocean floor, like the land, has its mountains, valleys, gorges, and rolling plains.

- [ ] Horatio Alger was the most prolific American author. He wrote, and had published, 119 full-length novels in thirty years.

- [ ] Philadelphia, Pennsylvania, has more individual homes than any other city in the world.

- [ ] The longest sermon on record was delivered by Clinton Locy of West Richland, Washington, in February 1955. It lasted forty-eight hours and eighteen minutes.

- [ ] The abbreviation *cir* before a date means the date cannot be fixed exactly.
- [ ] Cleopatra was of Greek ancestry and an Egyptian only by birth. She had no Egyptian blood in her veins.
- [ ] The approximate weight of a cubic foot of fresh water is 62.4 pounds.
- [ ] There is no federal law forbidding the total destruction of coins by owners, but mutilation is forbidden.
- [ ] A "printer's devil" is the newest apprentice in a printing shop.
- [ ] The world's largest baby whale weighed four tons.
- [ ] Mrs. Rebecca Felton of Georgia was the first woman to serve in the United States Senate.
- [ ] Nearly one million women in the United States go hunting.
- [ ] An area of two square feet and one of two feet square are not the same. The latter is twice as large as the former.
- [ ] Flax is harvested once in seven years.
- [ ] A baby kangaroo is carried in a pouch in the mother's abdomen.
- [ ] Billy Sunday, the world-famous evangelist, preached his last sermon October 27, 1935, and died on November 4, 1935.
- [ ] The ostrich covers twenty-five feet in one stride.
- [ ] Radio waves are believed to travel with the speed of light—about 167,227 miles a second.
- [ ] Mercury is the smallest of the planets. It is less than half the earth's size.
- [ ] The American Telephone and Telegraph Company is the largest corporation in the world.
- [ ] There is no appreciable decrease or increase in the weight of the human body after instant death occurs.
- [ ] Queen Anne, who ruled over England from 1702 to 1714, gave birth to seventeen children, not one of whom survived her.
- [ ] The island of Java, in the Netherlands East Indies, is the most densely populated country on earth. It has 860 people to every square mile.
- [ ] Alligators seldom viciously attack man either in or out of the water except in self-defense.
- [ ] As carriers of disease, rats have probably been responsible for more human deaths than all the wars of history.
- [ ] The weight of a grown mountain lion is about 180 pounds.
- [ ] Approximately four hundred dresses can be made from the average bale of cotton.
- [ ] The Bible was the first book that Abraham Lincoln learned to read.

- [ ] There is only one solution to the highway traffic problem—open our highways only to cars that are paid for.

- [ ] The slogan of the Salvation Army is, "A man may be down, but he's never out."

- [ ] A banana stalk produces only one bunch of bananas in a season.

- [ ] Henry Ford's father was a farmer in the state of Michigan.

- [ ] Dew does not fall from the sky as is popularly believed. Dew is water condensed on objects near the ground.

- [ ] The sun rises and sets only once each year at the North and South poles.

- [ ] On the occasion of a second marriage, the bride never wears a veil, nor does she dress in white.

- [ ] Elephants can swim, and they like water.

- [ ] The first daily newspaper in the United States made its appearance on September 21, 1784.

- [ ] President Franklin Pierce "said grace" before every meal and would transact no business nor open his mail on Sunday.

- [ ] Raw material for shellac comes from an insect that lives in some of the oriental countries.

- [ ] On August 30, in the year 30 B.C., Cleopatra committed suicide by permitting an asp to bite her.

- [ ] The finest powder produced is aluminum dust.

- [ ] In 1790, the first United States census showed a population of 3,929,214 persons in the thirteen states.

- [ ] The distance of the world's longest continuous railroad is fifty-eight hundred miles, from Leningrad to Vladivostok, Russia.

- [ ] Gypsies speak the Romany language, comprising about five thousand words.

- [ ] Water, when taken with meals, is an aid to the digestive process as long as the food is chewed properly.

- [ ] In Australia, there are thirteen sheep to every one person.

- [ ] Women have a higher incidence of tooth decay than do men.

- [ ] Captain Robert Gray, the discoverer of the Columbia River, was the first man to circumnavigate the globe under the American flag.

- [ ] Three out of every ten persons involved in a motor vehicle accident requires hospitalization.

- [ ] Woodrow Wilson was the only president of the United States who had a Ph.D. degree.

- [ ] More notes can be produced on the four strings of a violin than on the eighty-eight keys of a piano.

- [ ] "Crocodile tears" are hypocritical tears or pretended grief.

- [ ] The Japanese do not attach great importance to birthdays. They regard a child as being one year old when it is born.
- [ ] There is no difference in the kind of gas that is used in making carbonated drinks and dry ice.
- [ ] Louisiana is the wettest state in the United States.
- [ ] The country of Greenland covers 840,000 square miles.
- [ ] Botanically, the tomato is a fruit.
- [ ] A man equipped with a diving suit can go no farther down into the ocean than 360 feet and come up alive.
- [ ] Colonel E. S. Drake, a retired railroad conductor, is regarded as the father of the modern petroleum industry.
- [ ] It is believed that Dr. Oliver Wendell Holmes coined the phrase *white plague* as a common name for tuberculosis.
- [ ] The United States flag is flown over the White House when the president is in residence; it is taken down when he leaves to be gone overnight.
- [ ] Rice is the food that is eaten by the largest portion of the human race.
- [ ] Warren G. Harding was the first president of the United States to ride in an automobile in his inaugural parade.
- [ ] The country of Denmark is about twice the size of the state of Massachusetts.
- [ ] In playing the game Tug of War, a team moves backward to win.
- [ ] Osmium is the heaviest metal on earth. A baseball made out of osmium would weigh more than forty regular baseballs.
- [ ] There were 61,825 homes destroyed when the atomic bomb was dropped on Hiroshima.
- [ ] More state names begin with *M* and *N* than with any other two letters.
- [ ] Under normal conditions, when a river is rising the water surface is higher at the center than at the sides.
- [ ] The tusks of an elephant continues to grow until the animal dies.
- [ ] London, England, was the first city in the world to attain a population of one million persons.
- [ ] The word *facade* is an architectural term for the external face of a building, especially the principal front.
- [ ] Faneuil Hall in Boston, Massachusetts, is often referred to as the ''Cradle of Liberty.''
- [ ] The president of the United States cannot veto the separate items in any bill sent to him by Congress.
- [ ] In China, everybody celebrates his birthday on New Year's Day.

- [ ] In carving meat, generally speaking, all carving should be across the grain, with the exception of steak.

- [ ] The letters *RX* on a doctor's prescription means "take."

- [ ] People chew gum when traveling by air because the working of the jaws tends to keep the air pressure equalized on both sides of the eardrums.

- [ ] A naturalized citizen has the same rights as one who is native born, except that he may not become president of the United States.

- [ ] The tallest tree in the world is 364 feet in height.

- [ ] In Tasmania, the natives know only three different numbers: one, two, and plenty.

- [ ] As a group, hawks seem to be the swiftest of all the bird family.

- [ ] The New York International Airport (Idlewild) is the largest commercial air terminal in the world, occupying forty-nine hundred acres of land.

- [ ] Beethoven, the noted German composer, dressed so shabbily that he was once arrested as a tramp.

- [ ] A person must be at least fifty-six feet from a wall or other reflecting objects in order to hear an echo.

- [ ] The term *United Kingdom* includes northern Ireland, while the term *Great Britain* does not.

- [ ] *Amen* means "so be it."

- [ ] There are more geysers in Yellowstone National Park than in all the rest of the world together.

- [ ] The first atomic-powered submarine was launched January 21, 1954.

- [ ] Sir Henry Dale, a British physician, discovered the fundamental causes of allergy, in 1910.

- [ ] Melodies are produced by notes in succession, harmonies by notes in combination.

- [ ] The Charter of the United Nations was signed on June 26, 1945, in San Francisco.

- [ ] A pig always sleeps on its right side.

- [ ] The bazooka, developed by the United States Army, was first used in 1942.

- [ ] President Benjamin Harrison was an elder in the Presbyterian Church for forty-seven years.

- [ ] About 40 percent of the people of the United States have a mental age of about thirteen.

- [ ] The highest natural temperature ever recorded was 136 degrees (in the shade) on September 13, 1922. The place was Azizia, North Africa.

☐ Figuero Street in Los Angeles, California, is the longest street in the world. It runs north and south through the city for a distance of thirty miles.

☐ "Reading the riot act" literally means to give warning to a crowd to disperse under penalty of law.

☐ A rattlesnake is dangerous from the moment of its birth.

☐ The solar system consists of the earth and the other eight planets, and their moons, or satellites.

☐ President James K. Polk was sprinkled on his death bed by a Methodist minister.

☐ "Podunk" is a humorous name for any small out-of-the-way country village or a jerkwater town.

☐ The largest fish that has ever been caught was a white shark weighing 2,176 pounds.

☐ Patrick Henry began his study of law only six weeks before he was admitted to the bar.

☐ There are three types of bees: queens, drones, and workers.

☐ Human taste buds are divided into four groups: those which respond to salt, those which respond to sweet, those which respond to sour, and those which respond to bitter substances.

☐ The Boy Scouts of America was incorporated in 1910, and chartered by Congress in 1916.

☐ Ulysses S. Grant was the only president of the United States to ever be arrested during his term of office. He was arrested for exceeding the speed limit while driving a team of spirited horses through the streets of Washington.

☐ A thick glass filled with hot liquid will be more likely to crack than a thin one.

☐ The first Cesarean operation performed in the United States in which both mother and child survived, was performed by Dr. John Lambert Richmond at Newton, Ohio, on April 22, 1827.

☐ Cellophane was first used on a large scale for wrapping cigarettes.

☐ Only 10 percent of American women can whistle.

☐ President Franklin D. Roosevelt and his wife were fifth cousins.

☐ Scripture records only one time that Jesus Christ admitted that He was the Messiah, and that was in a private conversation. See John 4:26.

☐ Ninety percent of all men's handkerchiefs sold in the United States each year are bought by women.

☐ President John Quincy Adams read the Bible through at least once each year.

☐ The average housewife will wash 2½ million cooking and eating utensils in her lifetime.

- [ ] Most snakes travel only a few miles from the place where they were born.

- [ ] "Alma Mater" is a Latin term (bounteous mother) applied by students to the college or university that they attended.

- [ ] Dolly Madison, wife of President James Madison, instituted the first inaugural ball at the White House.

- [ ] If marshmallows packed in tin cans were taken to a height above seven thousand feet, the lessened air pressure would cause the cans to explode.

- [ ] The duration of a copyright is twenty-eight years from the date of first application.

- [ ] Frogs and flies can catch athlete's foot the same as people.

- [ ] William F. Semple obtained the first patent on chewing gum at Mount Vernon, Ohio, in 1869.

- [ ] President Harry S. Truman had a horseshoe put up for luck over the main entrance to his White House office.

- [ ] The tropical American sloth is the laziest animal in the modern world.

- [ ] One jelly bean contains seven calories.

- [ ] Orville Wright made the first successful airplane flight December 17, 1903, at Kitty Hawk, North Carolina.

- [ ] The shadow of an airplane is always the same size, no matter how high or how low the plane flies.

- [ ] John Wesley, the noted Methodist minister, was born June 17, 1703.

- [ ] An owl's eyes do not move in their sockets.

- [ ] The game of basketball was invented by James Naismith of Springfield, Massachusetts, in 1891.

- [ ] Esther Cleveland was the only child of a president to be born in the White House.

- [ ] The hind footprints of a rabbit's track are ahead of the front footprints.

- [ ] It is possible for a fish to get seasick.

- [ ] No president of the United States has ever resigned, but biographers say that Woodrow Wilson contemplated doing so.

- [ ] The average ant is capable of crawling twelve feet a minute on a fast track.

- [ ] Charles R. DeVevoise produced the first brassiere in the United States, in 1904.

- [ ] Andrew Johnson was the only president of the United States to face impeachment proceedings. In 1868 he was tried by the Senate and acquitted by one vote.

- [ ] Technically, a goose is a female, the male being the gander.
- [ ] A football is made from cowhide, not from pigskin.
- [ ] The wife of President James Madison became famous as the best-dressed woman in Washington.
- [ ] United States Senator, Huey Long, made the longest speech in the Senate on record. He talked constantly for 15 ½ hours.
- [ ] About four hours are required to hardboil an ostrich egg.
- [ ] The Chinese discovered natural gas as early as 940 B.C.
- [ ] A large brain does not always indicate superior intelligence. The largest brain on record belonged to an unskilled laborer.
- [ ] President Andrew Jackson suffered from tuberculosis most of the time he was in the White House.
- [ ] The average length of the heart in adult human beings is about five inches.
- [ ] Buenos Aires, Argentina, is the largest city south of the equator.
- [ ] Slamming an oven door will cause a cake to fall because it breaks the tiny air cells in the cake.
- [ ] Liberia, the Negro republic in West Africa, uses an elephant as an emblem on its currency.
- [ ] All the states of the United States have stringent laws against dueling.
- [ ] The blood pressure of spiders is about the same as that of people.
- [ ] Practically all horseshoes are made of steel.
- [ ] The Shrine was organized by a group of Freemasons September 26, 1872, in New York City.
- [ ] One out of every twenty pigs now being slaughtered has an ulcer.
- [ ] Generals Lee and Grant met only one time after the surrender at Appomattox.
- [ ] The earliest recorded ballet performance took place in Milan, Italy, in 1489, at the wedding of the Duke of Milan to Isabel of Aragon.
- [ ] A very good way to find out whether or not an egg has been cooked is to attempt to spin it. A raw egg will not spin.
- [ ] Chester A. Arthur was the first president of the United States to smoke cigarettes.
- [ ] The average seven-inch lead pencil will draw a line thirty-five miles long.
- [ ] It takes more sugar to sweeten a cold drink than a hot drink.
- [ ] Crystal is the heaviest and most brilliant kind of glass.
- [ ] The coldest inhabited spot in the world is north central Siberia.
- [ ] It is true that most male hippopotami are "henpecked."

- [ ] If one spent at the rate of one dollar per minute, it would require approximately two thousand years to spend a billion dollars.

- [ ] All icebergs are not white. Some are green and some are black. Their color depends on age and place of origin.

- [ ] The average lifespan of a buzzard in captivity is thirty-two years.

- [ ] Reno, Nevada, is located farther west than Los Angeles, California.

- [ ] About seventy buttons a year are required by the average American.

- [ ] There is no such thing as absolutely pure drinking water.

- [ ] Four presidents of the United States were married twice: Millard Fillmore, Benjamin Harrison, Theodore Roosevelt, and Woodrow Wilson.

- [ ] If a morning glory is placed in a closet, it will open the following morning as if it were in the sun, but the second morning it will not open, because it can't be fooled again.

- [ ] The earthworm has no eyes, but it is able to perceive light through its skin.

- [ ] A rattlesnake holds its rattle above the water when swimming.

- [ ] It is possible for a river to flow away from its mouth. The Chicago River flows away from its mouth, due to an engineering feat.

- [ ] The largest artificial eye ever made was for a prize Hereford bull, by the American Optical Company.

- [ ] Airways over the United States are now numbered somewhat like highway routes. Odd-numbered airways run north and south, while even numbers designate east-west routes.

- [ ] God hates seven things. See Proverbs 6:16-19.

- [ ] Normal adults and growing children require one gram of protein daily for every 2.2 pounds of body weight.

- [ ] Eighteen newborn opossums can be placed in a teaspoon.

- [ ] The same amount of sweetening tastes sweeter at higher temperatures.

- [ ] Approximately sixteen thousand conventions of various kinds are held in the United States each year.

- [ ] No part of a snake's body leaves the ground when it moves from place to place.

- [ ] The length of a year on the planet Jupiter is twelve times the length of our year on earth.

- [ ] Sick plants run temperatures from one-tenth of one to two degrees centigrade higher than healthy ones.

- [ ] Woodrow Wilson, in a speech at the National Press Club of Washington, D.C., January 9, 1912, admitted he had a "single-track" mind.

- [ ] The extent of George Washington's formal education corresponded to about the fifth grade in a modern public school.

- [ ] Under normal conditions, the average person takes about seventeen breaths each minute.

- [ ] A catechism is any compendious system of teaching drawn up in the form of questions and answers.

- [ ] On May 20 and 21, 1927, Charles Lindbergh flew from New York to Paris, France, a distance of thirty-six hundred miles in 33½ hours.

- [ ] "Breach of promise" means the failure, deliberate or unintentional, to do any lawful thing which one has bound himself by contract to do.

- [ ] Thomas Jefferson owned ten thousand acres of land, and 130 slaves.

- [ ] The war between England and the United States ended December 24, 1814.

- [ ] Notaries public in the District of Columbia are appointed by the president of the United States.

- [ ] The diameter of the sun is 864,000 miles. The diameter of the earth is only 8,000 miles.

- [ ] It is possible for a frog to sing under water because they normally sing with their mouths and nostrils closed.

- [ ] John Tyler was elected sheriff of Saint Charles County, Virginia, after retiring from the presidency.

- [ ] Only 5 percent of the people of the United States dream in color.

- [ ] The first daily mail service by airplane was inaugurated May 15, 1918, between New York City and Washington.

- [ ] Fish are able to tell the difference between red and green lights.

- [ ] Noah Webster spent twenty years in making his famous dictionary of the English language.

- [ ] The highest wind velocity ever recorded in the United States is 231 miles per hour.

- [ ] Leeward is the direction *to* which wind is blowing. Windward is the direction *from* which wind is blowing.

- [ ] An ear of corn always has an even number of rows of kernels.

- [ ] The average soldier of World War II was three-quarters of an inch taller than the average soldier of World War I.

- [ ] Pythagoras, a Greek philosopher who lived in the sixth century B.C., was the first to conceive of the earth as a globe.

- [ ] Mosquitoes dislike citronella because it irritates their feet.

- [ ] The flamingo remains in a standing position a larger proportion of its life than any other known bird. It sits down only when it nests or bathes.

- [ ] Men have been writing checks for at least twenty-seven hundred years.

- [ ] The Fiji Islands in the South Pacific has the healthiest climate in the world. The temperature there has never gone below sixty-three degrees, nor above ninety.

- [ ] Chester A. Arthur, president of the United States, employed a personal valet who brushed his clothes, shaved him, and trimmed his fingernails and toenails.

- [ ] Three different countries conduct a census every ten years: Canada, Great Britain, and the United States.

- [ ] Dr. Daniel David Palmer discovered the science of chiropractic in Davenport, Iowa, in 1895.

- [ ] If a child ate as much, comparatively, as a growing bird, he would consume three lambs and one calf in a single day.

- [ ] Henry Ford, of automobile fame, originally planned to manufacture cheap watches on a large scale as a means of livelihood.

- [ ] Cows which have access to water twenty-four hours a day drink about a third of their intake at night.

- [ ] The smallest church building in the world is located on the outskirts of Covington, Kentucky. It accommodates only three worshipers.

- [ ] Malaysia is the world's largest rubber producer.

- [ ] Grover Cleveland held the office of sheriff of Erie County, New York, before becoming president of the United States.

- [ ] The basic explosive in dynamite is nitroglycerin.

- [ ] Dr. Crawford Long is said to have been the first American physician to use ether as an anesthetic in a surgical operation.

- [ ] The city of Venice, Italy, is built on about 120 small, mud islands.

- [ ] Thirty-seven and one half pounds of sulphur are required to manufacture one ton of newsprint.

- [ ] In 1912, the first Chamber of Commerce in the United States was organized.

- [ ] Rhode Island was the first of the original American colonies to declare independence from Great Britain.

- [ ] President Thomas Jefferson wrote his own epitaph, specified the size and material of his tombstone, and chose the exact spot for his grave.

- [ ] Two different kinds of sugar are found in honey: dextrose and levulose.

- [ ] In 1778, Francis Bailey, an almanac publisher in Lancaster, Pennsylvania, first referred to George Washington as "The Father of His Country."

- [ ] The down from forty cashmere goats is required to produce enough material for one overcoat.

☐ In the United States there are about twenty-five stillbirths for every thousand babies born alive.

☐ At a depth of 160 feet, a sea diver breathes five times as much oxygen as he normally does.

☐ The first performance of a flea circus took place in 1846, under the august sponsorship of King Louis Phillippe, of France.

☐ Spots and lines appearing on the fingernails indicate imperfections in the nails.

☐ There are from five to eight hundred vines per acre in the average vineyard.

☐ Camp Fire Girls was founded in 1910 by Dr. and Mrs. Luther Gulick.

☐ On a per ounce basis, a woman's swimsuit is the highest priced piece of wearing apparel in the United States.

☐ Striped barber poles are a relic of the days when barbers were also surgeons.

☐ Camphor is a product of the camphor tree, an evergreen found in China and Japan.

☐ The Bible prescribes death as the penalty for kidnaping. See Exodus 21:16.

☐ President Andrew Jackson joined the Presbyterian Church the year following his retirement.

☐ Buzzards possess keen eyesight. They are able to discover even a small animal from a height of one thousand feet or more.

☐ The Caspian Sea, with an estimated area of 168,765 square miles, is the largest inland body of water in the world.

☐ Penicillin was first produced synthetically in a laboratory in 1946.

☐ In the United States, one person in twenty suffer from some form of rheumatism.

☐ The ear helps us to keep our balance.

☐ President Rutherford B. Hayes was the first president to ban liquor in the White House.

☐ A "whipping boy" is a scapegoat, one punished for the short-comings of another.

☐ Stephen Foster, famed writer of songs, died a pauper and an alcoholic at the age of thirty-eight.

☐ The yellow stain from cigarettes is caused by tar oil in cigarette smoke.

☐ A female sea horse does not possess a pouch, but the male does.

☐ The longest highway across the United States, Highway 66, is 3,652 miles long.

☐ Gypsum is a crystalline rock made up of calcium and sulphur.

- [ ] President Theodore Roosevelt was once a cowpuncher.

- [ ] Growing peas will increase nearly 50 percent in weight between 5 A.M. and sunset in a single good growth day.

- [ ] A tree must be at least ten feet high. A shrub is less than ten feet high.

- [ ] The president of Switzerland holds office for a period of one year.

- [ ] Alcohol is not fattening. The calories in alcohol cannot be stored in the body as fat.

- [ ] In politics, a "dark horse" is a little known person who gets a nomination unexpectedly.

- [ ] George Washington suffered greatly from dental troubles. He was fitted with a set of artificial teeth made of rhinoceros ivory.

- [ ] All crows are not black. The Clark crow is gray and white with black trimmings.

- [ ] President Chester A. Arthur gave his wife flowers every day of their married life, and after her death, placed fresh flowers before her portrait each day until stricken with his own fatal illness.

- [ ] The venomous rattlesnake always gives warning before it strikes.

- [ ] Cowards were exempt from military service in the ancient Jewish army. See Deuteronomy 20:1, 2, 8.

- [ ] Nature provides salt in three different forms: in sea water solution, in salt springs, and in the form of salt rock.

- [ ] The textile made from flax is called *linen*.

- [ ] Herbert Hoover and his wife were married by a Catholic priest because there was no Protestant minister available.

- [ ] More than twenty thousand men were killed, wounded, or missing in action in the Battle of Antietam, September 17, 1862. This was the bloodiest one-day fighting during the Civil War.

- [ ] Brisket is the breast of beef.

- [ ] Naturalists are inclined to believe that no animals are voiceless.

- [ ] About 740 chemicals of various kinds are now used to process, enrich, and preserve food.

- [ ] The width of the standard gauge railroad is 4 feet, 8½ inches, measured from the inside of one rail to the inside of the other.

- [ ] There is a bird so strong that it can break a man's arm with its wing. It is the swan.

- [ ] The dome of the state capitol in Frankfort, Kentucky, is modeled after the dome over Napoleon's tomb.

- [ ] Small loan companies make most of their loans for medical payments.

- [ ] No man has ever turned down the nomination for the presidency after it was made by a majority party.

- [ ] If the human body becomes saturated with iodine, there is an increase of moisture in the nose.

- [ ] Anne Boleyn, second wife of King Henry VIII, was deformed by the presence of an extra finger.

- [ ] President William Howard Taft initiated the custom of pitching the first ball at the opening of the baseball season in Washington, D.C.

- [ ] Until 1896, England had a law prohibiting any power-driven vehicle from traveling over four miles an hour on the public highways.

- [ ] The longest day in each year preceding a leap year is June 22, while in all other years it is June 21.

- [ ] In 1849, Elizabeth Blackwell became the first American woman physician with a regular medical degree and license.

- [ ] Franklin D. Roosevelt served as president of the United States for twelve years, one month, and eight days.

- [ ] The Suez Canal was officially opened November 17, 1869.

- [ ] Out of every dollar spent by American families for the care of their health, the medical profession receives thirty cents.

- [ ] In 1892, Steinmetz, an American scientist, discovered the laws of alternating current.

- [ ] The Hindu holy day begins at sunrise, the Jewish holy day at sunset, and the Christian holy day at midnight.

- [ ] Alcoholism is the fourth-ranking cause of insanity in the United States.

- [ ] A calf is born with four stomachs.

- [ ] The first vaudeville theater, the Gaiety, was opened for business in Boston, Massachusetts, in 1883.

- [ ] With an average altitude of only about sixty feet, Delaware is the lowest state in the United States.

- [ ] Miss Mary Katherine Goddard was the first woman to be post-mistress in the United States. She was postmistress of Baltimore, Maryland, from 1775 to 1789.

- [ ] The bat is the only mammal that can actually fly.

- [ ] Glass has a great resistance to crushing pressure. Its strength is greater than that of granite, concrete, clay brick, or even cast iron.

- [ ] Green is the most soothing color in the spectrum.

- [ ] One of the oldest means of therapy was massage or "laying on of hands."

- [ ] A beverage becomes an alcoholic beverage when it contains more than one-half of 1 percent alcohol by volume.

- [ ] President Woodrow Wilson was the author of the statement, "Politics is adjourned." He made the statement on May 27, 1918, in an address delivered to a joint session of Congress.

- [ ] The mackerel must swim constantly in order to live.
- [ ] Almost the entire earth's supply of iodine comes from the sea.
- [ ] Dreams do not foretell the future as is popularly believed.
- [ ] An idea cannot be patented.
- [ ] Housewives can get left-handed measuring cups if they so desire.
- [ ] The upper half of a parrot's beak is hinged and moves independently of the lower jaw.
- [ ] It has never been proved that opposites attract each other to marry.
- [ ] The Eiffel Tower in Paris, France, is 984 feet high.
- [ ] A normal, healthy person moves in his sleep about once every seven or eight minutes.
- [ ] There are approximately sixty active volcanoes in the world.
- [ ] The cat is the only domestic animal not mentioned in the Bible.
- [ ] Man has never been able to create a perfect vacuum, only partial vacuums.
- [ ] If the sun stopped shining suddenly, it would take eight minutes for people on the earth to become aware of the fact.
- [ ] The first European university was established at Salerno, Italy, in the ninth century.
- [ ] Among women, poisoning is the most common method of suicide.
- [ ] Mozart, the noted Austrian composer, began to compose at the age of five.
- [ ] The eye is quicker than the ear.
- [ ] Approximately fifty billion people have lived on this earth since the days of Christ.
- [ ] There is one liquor outlet for every four hundred persons in America.
- [ ] Wabash, Indiana, was the first city in the world to be lighted by electricity.
- [ ] Scientists cannot reliably predict earthquakes.
- [ ] Imprisonment for debt was abolished in the United States in 1798.
- [ ] The average life of a female deer is from eight to twelve years.
- [ ] Five hundred and eighty-four people lost their lives when the Iroquois Theater burned in 1923.
- [ ] There are two kinds of electricity: positive and negative.
- [ ] It takes forty thousand silkworm eggs to weigh one ounce.
- [ ] Clouds can be seen not more than thirty or forty miles in open, flat country.
- [ ] The four designated types of human blood are: A, B, AB, and O.

- [ ] *Uncle Tom's Cabin* was first published in 1852.
- [ ] It has not been proved that fish bite more readily in certain kinds of weather than in others.
- [ ] The District of Columbia was established by Congress July 16, 1790, with Washington, D.C. as the permanent capital of the United States.
- [ ] The year 1 B.C. preceded the year A.D. 1.
- [ ] At one time Jesus Christ was very unpopular in His hometown. See Luke 4:16-29.
- [ ] The women of Iceland keep their own names after marriage.
- [ ] President James Monroe, in 1820, received the largest percentage of the electoral vote of any United States president—231 out of 232.
- [ ] A meter is more than three inches longer than a yard.
- [ ] The actual explosion of an atomic bomb is over in less than a millionth of a second.
- [ ] A mother does not have anything to do with determining the sex of her child.
- [ ] There are about four miles of thread in a pair of women's stockings.
- [ ] A woman is always *presented*, not *introduced*, to the president of the United States.
- [ ] The Atlantic Ocean is deeper than the Pacific Ocean by 216 feet.
- [ ] Cutting the hair does not make it grow faster.
- [ ] There are more than fourteen thousand women's clubs in the United States.
- [ ] The famous Casey Jones was connected with the Mississippi division of the Illinois Central Railroad.
- [ ] Water is the greatest solvent.
- [ ] Virginia, with an area of 64,284 square miles, was the largest of the thirteen original colonies.
- [ ] More earthquakes occur in Chile than in any other country; Japan ranks second.
- [ ] A human being has about 639 muscles.
- [ ] The penny is not the official and legal designation of any coin minted in the United States. It is merely a colloquial name for the American one-cent piece.
- [ ] Bridges and other steel structures are painted with red paint because as an anticorrosive it helps to prevent the formation of rust.
- [ ] Two hundred million atoms placed in a row would measure one inch.
- [ ] Water does not actually boil when dry ice is dropped into it.

- [ ] Bowling is the most popular nonspectator sport in the United States.

- [ ] The simplest way to remove old wallpaper from a wall is to soak it with water by steaming, then scrape.

- [ ] Santa Fe, New Mexico, founded in the winter of 1609-10 and named capital of the territory in 1851, retained its position as capital when New Mexico became a state, making it the oldest city in the United States to serve as capital of a state.

- [ ] Mrs. Eugenia Anderson was the first woman in the history of the United States to be appointed ambassador to a foreign country. She became ambassador to Denmark in 1949.

- [ ] Generally, a young woman is called a bride for one year after her marriage.

- [ ] The ocean is never perfectly calm.

- [ ] Worsteds are made from the longer fibers combed out of virgin wool, while woolens are made from short fibers.

- [ ] An average man can work at the rate of about one-tenth horse-power with his arms.

- [ ] One wild turkey requires a range of about twelve hundred acres.

- [ ] Los Angeles, California, was established in 1781 by forty-four settlers from Mexico.

- [ ] Thomas Jefferson was the first president of the United States to wear long trousers.

- [ ] The female buffalo in India gives richer milk than any domestic cow.

- [ ] At least some sugar is found in practically every food, including meat.

- [ ] Genghis Khan, Mongol conqueror, introduced the use of gun powder, when he invaded China in A.D. 1215.

- [ ] The height of the Boulder (Hoover) Dam is 727 feet.

- [ ] There are thirty-two teeth in a full set of adult teeth.

- [ ] Cancer of the throat caused the death of President Ulysses S. Grant.

- [ ] The famous Pony Express of the long ago was not operated by the United States government. It was a private enterprise.

- [ ] Ink used in printing has about the same consistency as molasses.

- [ ] A given quantity of water does not change its weight in the process of freezing.

- [ ] The most common poisonous snake in the United States is the copperhead. Its bite is not always fatal.

- [ ] Fifty men who signed the Declaration of Independence were Freemasons.

- [ ] The python can attain a length of thirty feet and a weight of three hundred pounds.

- [ ] The best method of peeling onions to prevent odor and smarting eyes is to peel them under water.

- [ ] Babies are born with the sense of touch, and the sense of smell develops immediately after birth.

- [ ] The Presbyterian Minister's Fund originated in 1759 was the first life insurance company to be chartered in America.

- [ ] There are thirty basic groups of plastics.

- [ ] In India, a man is specifically forbidden to marry his great-grandmother.

- [ ] Napoleon Bonaparte originated the idea of odd and even numbers on different sides of the street.

- [ ] President George Washington's second inaugural address was noted for its brevity. It contained only 134 words.

- [ ] The cigar lighter was patented by Moses F. Gale of New York City, November 21, 1871.

- [ ] Vermont was the first state to be admitted to the United States after the original thirteen.

- [ ] Three billion, two hundred million acres of the earth's surface is covered with sand dunes.

- [ ] In 1825, John Stevens of Hoboken, New Jersey, built the first steam locomotive in the United States to run on rails.

- [ ] The mouse is the most common mammal in the United States.

- [ ] Charcoal is used to cure tobacco, filter water, and make black jelly beans.

- [ ] From the top of the Empire State Building in New York City, one can see as far as fifty miles and into five states.

- [ ] The armistice ending the Korean War was signed July 27, 1953.

- [ ] The fragrance of flowers is due to the special essences of oil which the plants produce.

- [ ] Epsom salts takes its name from a mineral spring at Epsom, England.

- [ ] The world's largest office building is the Pentagon, in Washington, D.C.

- [ ] The weasel, a small, reddish brown animal, turns white in frigid, cold climates.

- [ ] The cheetah is the world's speediest four-legged animal.

- [ ] Celluloid was the first plastic; it was used to make billard balls.

- [ ] Thomas A. Edison has been called the greatest benefactor of humanity in modern times.

- [ ] Straight hair will not grow curly after the scalp has been shaved.
- [ ] The brain of a human being has twice as many nerve cells as that of the highest ape.
- [ ] Light travels at the rate of 186,200 miles a second.
- [ ] Although frost does not cause the chemical process that produces the brilliant colors in autumn leaves, it often hastens the coloring process.
- [ ] The population of the world is increasing at the rate of about five thousand every hour.
- [ ] It takes seven billion fog particles to make a teaspoon of water.
- [ ] The four fundamental units of human society are the home, the state, the church, and the school.
- [ ] It is estimated that the world's average rainfall is sixteen million tons per second.
- [ ] Two brothers, John and Charles Wesley, came to America as missionaries and became the founders of the Methodist Church.
- [ ] The cost of taking the first national census in 1790 was forty-four thousand dollars.
- [ ] Water literally runs off a duck's back.
- [ ] People continue to grow at the rate of nearly half an inch in twenty years after full normal growth has been attained.
- [ ] Martin Van Buren and Chester Arthur were considered the most polished of all the presidents of the United States.
- [ ] The largest bus terminal in the world is the Port Authority in New York City.
- [ ] Old Faithful, a geyser in Yellowstone Park, erupts approximately every sixty-five minutes.
- [ ] Unidentical twins are called fraternal twins.
- [ ] The bluebird is the official bird of the state of Missouri.
- [ ] Industrial life insurance had its beginning in November, 1875.
- [ ] A queen honeybee lays about fifteen hundred eggs each day during the summer.
- [ ] The easiest way to open a fruit jar is to turn it upside down in hot water. After a minute or two the metal top expands and loosens.
- [ ] One out of every one thousand children born is afflicted with mongalism.
- [ ] William Howard Taft was the only president of the United States who served both as president and chief justice of the Supreme Court.
- [ ] A seven-pound codfish can produce seven million eggs at a time.
- [ ] School chalk is not chalk. It's plaster of Paris.

- [ ] The narrowest part of the English Channel is about twenty miles wide.

- [ ] Dry cleaning is not dry. The articles are placed in a washer containing fluid and thoroughly saturated.

- [ ] About four hundred people died in the eastern United States during the Great Blizzard of 1888.

- [ ] The Pacific Ocean is less stormy than the Atlantic.

- [ ] Eleven generals have become president of the United States.

- [ ] Seventy percent of the liquor sold in this country is sold in package stores.

- [ ] The lowest point on the earth's surface is the Dead Sea, 1,290 feet below sea level.

- [ ] A twelve-ounce bottle of beer yields to its consumer seven calories of energy.

- [ ] On June 27, 1945, Premier Joseph Stalin, a self-made man, promoted himself to generalissimo.

- [ ] Twenty-six different breeds of cats are registered in Great Britain.

- [ ] The blowing of the wind has no effect upon a thermometer after the thermometer has once attained the temperature of the wind.

- [ ] A fly is not a fly, nor is a glowworm a worm. They're both beetles.

- [ ] According to the present accident rates in the United States, the average person will be seriously injured four times during his lifetime.

- [ ] The back part of the human tongue is the most sensitive to taste.

- [ ] Benjamin Rush is the father of American psychiatry.

- [ ] "Bonded whiskey" is straight whiskey of 100 proof, and must be at least four years old.

- [ ] In the country of Greece, 50 percent of the dentists are women.

- [ ] The normal life of a canary is about twenty years.

- [ ] In 1832, John C. Calhoun resigned as vice-president of the United States after he was elected to the Senate.

- [ ] In January of 1899, Humphrey O'Sullivan of Lowell, Massachusetts, patented the rubber heel.

- [ ] The average American drinks about fifty-two gallons of coffee each year.

- [ ] The term *eighteen-carat gold* means an alloy made up of 75 percent pure gold and 25 percent of some other metal.

- [ ] Queen Isabeau of France (1371-1435) was the first woman in recorded history to wear lingerie.

- [ ] On June 2, 1883, in Fort Wayne, Indiana, the first night baseball game was played.

- [ ] Lindsay, Oklahoma, is the largest broomcorn shipping point in the United States.

- [ ] Dreams usually last from ten to thirty minutes.

- [ ] The female flea, not the male, is trained for exhibition in circuses.

- [ ] Grover Cleveland was the only president of the United States to be married in the White House, June 2, 1886.

- [ ] A human being would have to walk approximately five miles to burn up the calories in a chocolate sundae.

- [ ] The Liberty Bell cracked in 1835 as it tolled for the funeral of John Marshall.

- [ ] John Sigmund of St. Louis, Missouri, swam nonstop down the Mississippi River for a distance of 292 miles in eighty hours and forty-eight minutes.

- [ ] A single pail of water can produce enough fog to cover 105 square miles to a depth of fifty feet.

- [ ] Magellan took thirty-five compasses on his round-the-world voyage.

- [ ] There are ten million bricks in the Empire State Building in New York City.

- [ ] The opossum, though slow and stupid, often feigns death when caught.

- [ ] J. Edgar Hoover was appointed director of the Federal Bureau of Investigation in 1924.

- [ ] In about 40 percent of all sterile marriages the cause lies with the husband.

- [ ] There are at least thirty-four active volcanoes in Alaska.

- [ ] The average American adult reads at a speed of 150 to 200 words a minute.

- [ ] Millard Fillmore and Warren G. Harding were considered the most handsome of all the presidents of the United States.

- [ ] A mosquito bite is not a bite. It is a puncture.

- [ ] Man can look the longest at the colors blue and green.

- [ ] The favorite amusement of automobile magnate Henry Ford in his youth was to take a watch apart and put it back together.

- [ ] The alcoholic content of natural wines never exceeds 14 percent.

- [ ] Quadruplets occur only once in every million confinements.

- [ ] In India, the life expectancy is 32½ years.

- [ ] At 150 feet above sea level, the horizon is just fifteen miles away.

- [ ] There are only seven thousand miles of railroads in Belgium.

- [ ] Among men, firearms is the most common method of suicide.

- [ ] George Washington began his career as a surveyor in 1748, at Winchester, Virginia.

- [ ] Whales are able to swim at a speed of up to twenty miles an hour.

- [ ] During his lifetime, Andrew Carnegie gave away nearly a third of a billion dollars.

- [ ] The composition of the human body and the composition of seven gallons of seawater are the same.

- [ ] The guinea pig is very sensitive to toxins and poisons.

- [ ] Vaughan DeLeath, a radio singer, was the first to introduce a type of singing called "crooning" (October 11, 1921).

- [ ] The silk worm is not a worm. It is a caterpillar.

- [ ] A beech tree can consume more than fifty gallons of water per day.

- [ ] Five feet, five inches is the average height of American women.

- [ ] Three hundred thousand pencils can be made from the average cedar tree.

- [ ] The figurative term *seven seas* denotes all the seas and oceans of the world.

- [ ] In 1892, Charles E. Duryea, of Springfield, Massachusetts, manufactured the first automobile in the United States.

- [ ] One hundred forty-six Union soldiers were hanged for desertion during the Civil War.

- [ ] Synthetic rubber is superior to the natural product in resisting oils, chemicals, heat, and cold.

- [ ] The largest elephant tusk on record measured eleven feet, five and one-half inches in length and eighteen inches in circumference at its girth.

- [ ] In human beings it takes a nerve impulse about eight one-thousandths of a second to reach the brain.

- [ ] Handling a toad will not give a person warts, as some seem to believe.

- [ ] Harry S. Truman was the first president of the United States to veto a tax reduction bill.

- [ ] An estimated 8 percent of the men in the United States are color-blind.

- [ ] Eastport, Maine, is the easternmost city in the United States.

- [ ] It takes one year for the fruit of the coconut tree to ripen.

- [ ] One hundred and eighty-one different women are mentioned by name in the Bible.

- [ ] The average human being can run about twenty miles an hour.

- [ ] In playing poker, there is one chance in five hundred of drawing a flush.

- [ ] In proportion to its size, the ant has the largest brain in the animal kingdom.

- [ ] John Wanamaker was the first merchant in the United States to insert full-page advertisements in a newspaper.

- [ ] The anemometer is an instrument which measures the force, velocity, or pressure of the wind.

- [ ] Usually it is easier to teach the male parrot to talk than the female.

- [ ] *Gone with the Wind* was the best selling novel this country has seen.

- [ ] The people of the state of Nevada are more inclined to kill themselves than those of other states.

- [ ] Bronze is an alloy of copper and tin.

- [ ] Thirty states in the United States prohibit the marriage of first cousins.

- [ ] On December 11, 1919, a monument was erected and dedicated to the boll weevil in the little town of Enterprise, Alabama.

- [ ] Andrew Jackson carved his name in a cave on Lookout Mountain in 1833.

- [ ] There are three viruses that cause polio.

- [ ] The odds are thirty-three to one against parents having a mentally retarded child.

- [ ] A piece of charcoal will absorb all odors if placed in a refrigerator.

- [ ] On June 11, 1657, Thomas Blake became the first preacher in the world to be addressed as "Reverend."

- [ ] House mice can run approximately four miles an hour.

- [ ] In the Belgian Congo, a chief's grave is marked by all the gin bottles he emptied during his lifetime.

- [ ] About 10 percent of white Americans have B-type blood.

- [ ] James A. Garfield was probably the most scholarly of all the presidents of the United States.

- [ ] One baby in one thousand is born with harelip.

- [ ] A person swimming in the Dead Sea cannot sink or completely submerge himself.

- [ ] The first "soda pop" was made in 1807.

- [ ] There is a much higher percentage of snorers among girls who smoke than those who don't.

- [ ] Abraham Lincoln and Charles Darwin were the children of cousin-marriages.

- [ ] Gold was discovered on the property of John A. Sutter in California on January 24, 1848. This led to the Gold Rush and the Forty-Niners.

- [ ] About one person in each 250 in the United States is afflicted with some form of epilepsy.

- [ ] The phrases *patent pending* and *patent applied for* have no legal significance.

- [ ] Elephants do not grow as tall as is generally believed. A specimen more than ten feet tall at the shoulders would be regarded as an extemely tall animal.

- [ ] On March 31, 1917, the United States bought the Virgin Islands from Denmark for twenty-five million dollars.

- [ ] Ulcers are more prevalent in the thin, wiry man engaged in some mental occupation.

- [ ] The typewritter ribbon was patented by George K. Anderson of Memphis, Tennessee, on September 14, 1886.

- [ ] Some hens lay more than two hundred eggs in a season if they are promptly taken away as they are laid.

- [ ] The lungs of a man are able to hold twice as much air as that of a whale.

- [ ] All our physical characteristics are determined by the genes which we inherit from our parents.

- [ ] Warren G. Harding, in June 21, 1923, became the first president of the United States to speak over the radio.

- [ ] Quarters are the most sought after coins in New York State.

- [ ] A bear cub at birth weighs only about twelve or fourteen ounces.

- [ ] It was General Phillip H. Sheridan who said, "If I owned Texas and hell, I would rent out Texas and live in hell."

- [ ] Cards that have stamps printed on them and that are sold by a post office are properly called postal cards. Unstamped cards sold by private firms are properly called postcards.

- [ ] Monkeys, like human beings, grow a second set of teeth.

- [ ] Barbed wire was first manufactured in 1873.

- [ ] A president of the United States has been born in every month of the year except June.

- [ ] There are more than thirty species of buzzards.

- [ ] Louisiana is the only state whose laws are not based on English common law.

- [ ] The bones of fish are softened by heat, not by oil, as popularly supposed.

- [ ] From the standpoint of eugenics and biology, brothers and sisters bear a closer relationship to one another than they do to either of their parents.

- [ ] Ann Boleyn, the second wife of King Henry VIII, was beheaded on May 19, 1536. The king charged her with adultery.

- [ ] Astronaut Edwin E. "Buzz" Aldrin, Jr. was the first Master Mason to set foot on the moon.

- [ ] Banana stalks are not trees in the correct sense of the term. They are large perennial herbs that reach their full growth in one season.

- [ ] The element nitrogen is the lightest substance known to science.

- [ ] In 1828, the Russian government began the coinage of platinum money because the metal was produced in considerable quantities in that country.

- [ ] President Calvin Coolidge had the oath of office administered to him by his father.

- [ ] On May 25, 1935, Babe Ruth hit his 714th (and last) home run.

- [ ] A fog is merely condensed water vapor and differs from a cloud in that it is closer to the ground.

- [ ] It is estimated that there are from fourteen to eighteen square feet of skin on the average adult human body.

- [ ] A fat person floats more readily in water than a lean person. In proportion to size, a fat person is lighter than a lean one.

- [ ] Although diamond is crystal clear, when reduced to dust it is as black as other carbon. A diamond is the only gem composed of only one element.

- [ ] Fish are unable to close their eyes and do not sleep in the ordinary sense of that term as applied to mammals.

- [ ] Pure radium resembles common table salt.

- [ ] The law of gravitation was discovered in 1687.

- [ ] Onions actually have no taste at all. We smell onions rather than taste them.

- [ ] Elephants reach maturity at about thirty-five, and begin to get old at sixty or sixty-five.

- [ ] Abdalah, the father of Mohammed, was so strikingly handsome that when he married the hearts of two hundred virgins were broken from disappointed love.

- [ ] At atmosphere pressure, dry ice has a temperature of nearly 110 degrees below zero, or 140 degrees lower than natural or artificial ice.

- [ ] Ostriches are essentially vegetarians. In captivity their food consists of alfalfa hay, wheat, bran, barley, oats, and fresh greens. They eat some insects and occasionally small mammals.

- [ ] Two nails driven into a tree trunk, one above the other, will remain the same distance apart as the tree grows.

- [ ] The frog does not breathe like most air breathing animals—the air must be swallowed in order to be conveyed to the lungs.

- [ ] At least ten different species of salmon are known to exist.

- [ ] In the political sense, a "slush fund" is a campaign fund collected to influence public opinion by improper means.

- [ ] Helium weighs about one-seventh as much as air.

- [ ] Baking powder produces many tiny bubbles in a cake which causes it to rise to the desired degree.

- [ ] There is more moonlight in autumn than at any other time of the year.

- [ ] Cardinal Mezzofanti (1774-1849) spoke sixty languages fluently.

- [ ] Red cedar is highly preferred for making lead pencils because it does not splinter.

- [ ] All bananas are picked green. They are not fit to eat if permitted to ripen on the plants.

- [ ] A parrot can learn to "speak" one language as well as another.

- [ ] At a wedding breakfast, the best man serves as toastmaster.

- [ ] President James A. Garfield was a member of the United States House of Representatives, senator-elect, and president-elect all at the same time for a period of four days.

- [ ] One half of 1 percent of the marriages in the United States are cousin marriages.

- [ ] John Oglethorpe founded the city of Savannah, Georgia, on February 12, 1733.

- [ ] Street letter boxes for depositing mail were in use in Belgium as early as 1848.

- [ ] For the first time in recorded history, on March 29, 1848, Niagara Falls stopped flowing. This was caused by an ice jam in the river above.

- [ ] A neurotic person is one suffering from a mental disturbance which handicaps but does not incapacitate him.

- [ ] Out of twenty gout patients, nineteen are men.

- [ ] Each female Japanese beetle lays about fifty eggs in her lifetime.

- [ ] The color red does not excite bulls—for the simple reason that they are color-blind.

- [ ] Animals exhale carbon dioxide which plants need and plants give off oxygen which animals need.

- [ ] On the darkest of nights, the rattlesnake can "see" a mouse or squirrel by the heat of its body.

- [ ] Governor John Winthrop, on June 25, 1620, introduced the table fork to America.

- [ ] On March 11, 1810, Napoleon was married by proxy to Mary Louise, daughter of Emperor Francis I of Austria. Napoleon was too busy to attend his wedding in person.

- [ ] The scales of a fish grow out from its body like shingles on a house.

- [ ] Jonas Bronck bought what is now known as the Bronx from the Indians in 1639, for "two guns, two kettles, two coats, two shirts, one barrel of cider, and six bits of money."

- [ ] Some baby giraffes are more than six feet tall at birth.

- [ ] The average salinity of Great Salt Lake, Utah, is almost six times greater than that of the oceans. No fish can live in such water.

- [ ] Spiders cannot be classified as insects. They have no "feelers" such as all insects have.

- [ ] The United States government disposes of its worn-out flags by burning them.

- [ ] Air that is thirty to forty feet above the ground is usually five to ten degrees warmer than the air just above the ground.

- [ ] One horsepower is equal to 746 watts. One kilowatt equals one thousand watts.

- [ ] The Arabians do all their reading and writing from right to left.

- [ ] If hogs are extemely fat, they are likely to scratch their throats while swimming and cause themselves to bleed to death.

- [ ] Clouds are nothing more than accumulations of mist.

- [ ] The massive organ in the Salt Lake City Mormon Temple has 10,804 pipes.

- [ ] A fly's taste buds are located in his feet.

- [ ] Homogenization of milk, contrary to popular belief, does not increase its nutritional value.

- [ ] Thunder is merely a secondary effect. It results from air rushing into the vacuum caused by a bolt of lightning.

- [ ] The Negro spirituals are remarkable in that, though born in slavery, they contain no note of bitterness.

- [ ] Penicillin is an organic compound consisting of carbon, hydrogen, oxygen, sulphur, and nitrogen.

- [ ] Salt in the pure state pours as easily in damp weather as in dry.

- [ ] Despite its great length, the neck of a giraffe is not long enough to reach the ground.

- [ ] Opossums are very prolific; females have been known to give birth to three litters in the same year.

- [ ] Theodore Roosevelt, at forty-two, was the youngest man to be inaugurated president of the United States.

- [ ] Sweets sometimes cause a toothache because of the ability of sugar solutions to extract water from the nerve of the tooth.

- [ ] The merry-go-round was patented by Wilhelm Schneider of Davenport, Iowa, on July 25, 1871.

- [ ] Squirrels habitually and naturally come down trees headfirst.

- [ ] Waterspouts at sea are composed chiefly of fresh water, not salt water as commonly supposed.

- [ ] Napoleon crowned himself emperor of France.

- [ ] The first India paper was made in 1875, by the Oxford University paper mills.

- [ ] Cows trained to be milked from one side often resent being milked from the other side.

- [ ] Lightning strikes upward as often as it does downward.

- [ ] In fish, the nostrils are used strictly for smelling and have no connection at all with breathing.

- [ ] The watermelon is said to be the only important fruit or vegetable from which no by-products are obtained.

- [ ] A midget is a person who, owing to supposedly faulty glands, virtually stops growing at a certain point in childhood but is normal in all other aspects.

- [ ] The apertures of the eyes of Chinese and Japanese are no more slanted than those of Caucasians.

- [ ] A bird swallows food without chewing it and it is ground by gravel in the gizzard.

- [ ] Thomas A. Edison invented the flashlight in 1914.

- [ ] In July, A.D. 64, two-thirds of Rome was destroyed by a fire that burned for nine days.

- [ ] Live mice cannot be shipped via United States mail.

- [ ] Neither birds nor snakes act naturally in captivity.

- [ ] Robert Burns and Napoleon were both habitual snuff users.

- [ ] Quinine, one of the most important drugs known to man, is obtained from the dried bark of an evergreen tree native to South America.

- [ ] The ukelele, essentially a small guitar with only four strings, is not of native Hawaiian origin as is commonly supposed. It was introduced to the Hawaiians by Portuguese sailors in the latter part of the eighteenth century.

- [ ] On February 17, 1876, the first sardine was canned at Eastport, Maine.

- [ ] It is impossible for a human being to reproduce exactly the tone of a bird.

- [ ] On September 3, 1883, the *New York Sun* became the first successful daily newspaper to sell for a penny.

- [ ] Hyman L. Lipman of Philadelphia, Pennsylvania patented a pencil with an eraser, on March 30, 1853.

- [ ] The peba, a small armadillo, bears its young in litters of four and the members of any given litter are invariably of the same sex.

☐ Kentucky still accounts for more than half of the whiskey production in the United States.

☐ President William Howard Taft was so tone deaf that he couldn't recognize the national anthem, and had his secretary nudge him so he could know when to rise when it was played at public functions.

☐ The United States government neither pays or receives a premium on any issue of coins or paper money, domestic or foreign.

☐ Panama hats are not made in Panama, as the name suggests, but in Ecuador, where their manufacture is a major industry.

☐ Chocolate differs from cocoa in being richer in fat and somewhat harder to prepare. Both are made from the seeds or beans of the cacao plant, an evergreen tree native to tropical America.

☐ The heart of a newborn baby beats about twice as fast as that of an adult.

☐ On April 25, 1816, Lord Byron separated from his wife and left England, a social outcast, never to return.

☐ Although it is customary for a person to bear the name of his parents, he is under no legal obligation to do so.

☐ Hong Kong is not the name of a city in China, as many people suppose, but the name of an island and a territory near the mouth of the Canton River.

☐ Water tumbles over the precipices of Niagara Falls at the rate of 500,000 tons a minute.

☐ A camel can travel long distances without food or water primarily because of the fat that is stored up in the hump or humps.

☐ Noncancelled United States postage stamps embossed on envelopes or printed on postal cards are not valid when attached to other mail matter.

☐ Gum chewing is regarded as a harmless habit that relaxes the nerves, and aids digestion by increasing the flow of saliva.

☐ The first book with a preface in the modern sense was printed in Rome in 1469.

☐ Three presidents of the United States were the sons of clergymen: Chester A. Arthur, Grover Cleveland, and Woodrow Wilson.

☐ At the present time, Canada produces about 60 percent of the world's asbestos; the United States produces less than 5 percent.

☐ A temperature of about 125 degrees below zero is required to freeze pure alcohol.

☐ William H. Bonney (1859-1881), one of the most notorious outlaws of the southwest, was known as Billy the Kid because of his youthfulness.

☐ The common belief that the century plant habitually blossoms once in a hundred years is a myth.

- [ ] What we call the sky is merely the limit of our vision into the atmosphere. The sky, like the horizon, is always as far away as one can see.

- [ ] The oiuja board was invented by Isaac Fuld and his brother William, and was patented July 1, 1892.

- [ ] Many conservative Chinese in the United States and other foreign countries, return their dead to China because of their belief in ancestor worship.

- [ ] On October 2, 1882, William H. Vanderbilt, the railroad magnate, made the headlines with his famous remark, "The public be damned."

- [ ] The American moose, a native of North America, is the largest member of the deer family, living or extinct.

- [ ] A fish opens and closes his mouth to pass water through the gills to obtain oxygen. The action is part of the breathing operation.

- [ ] The "gray matter" represents about 38 percent of the total weight of the human brain.

- [ ] On April 3, 1776, Harvard University conferred the honorary degree of Doctor of Laws on General George Washington.

- [ ] An earthworm native to southeastern Australia attains an extreme length of ten or twelve feet, and a diameter of three-fourths of an inch. The average specimen is only three or four feet long.

- [ ] Cooking utensils were first made of aluminum in 1892.

- [ ] Many species of snakes eat hens' eggs by swallowing them whole; in fact, that is the only way the snakes can eat them.

- [ ] In continental United States, pineapples are produced commercially only in Florida. Eighty percent of the world's pineapple supply is produced in Hawaii.

- [ ] By feeding hens certain dyes they can be made to lay eggs with varicolored yolks.

- [ ] A pint of oil will cover the surface of an acre of water.

- [ ] No species of wild plant produces a flower or blossom that is absolutely black, and so far none has been developed artificially.

- [ ] Pig iron is merely "raw iron" as it comes directly from the smelting furnace.

- [ ] Two presidents of the United States, James A. Garfield and Harry S. Truman, were born left-handed.

- [ ] The female tropical American sloth produces only one offspring in her lifetime.

- [ ] Libel is nothing more than written abuse.

- [ ] At its greatest depth the Pacific Ocean measures 36,201 feet deep.

- [ ] There are 10,221 contributors to the Encyclopaedia Britannica.

- [ ] In early Bible times, two sisters became the mothers of their half-brothers. See Genesis 19:30-38.

- [ ] To "eat humble pie" means to apologize, retract, recant, humiliate oneself, or eat one's words.

- [ ] Blue, black, and green ink are used in printing a United States one-dollar bill.

- [ ] The small intestines of a normal-sized man measures about twenty feet in length.

- [ ] The people of Hong Kong go to the movies more often than those of any other country in the world.

- [ ] England has had only one king who grew to manhood but never married. He was William II, son and successor of William the Conqueror.

- [ ] The record distance for a woman to throw a two-pound rolling pin is 137 feet, 6 inches. This feat was performed by Lindell Bowden of Australia, on July 22, 1967.

- [ ] Maryland has the only state flag bearing a coat of arms.

- [ ] Aaron Burr was the only vice-president of the United States chosen by the House of Representatives.

- [ ] The great water lily of the Amazon in South America has leaf blades up to five feet long.

- [ ] If your mouth were completely dry, you would not be able to taste anything.

- [ ] The sugar content of corn-on-the-cob drops rapidly after the corn is picked.

- [ ] Barring obstructions, at three feet above sea level one can see about 2 ¼ miles.

- [ ] Baylor University in Waco, Texas, is the largest Southern Baptist school in the world.

- [ ] The vicuna is the smallest of the camel family and, owing to its wild and active nature, it has never been domesticated.

- [ ] Between March 4, 1861, and January 18, 1862, five expresidents were living: Martin Van Buren, John Tyler, Millard Fillmore, Franklin Pierce, and James Buchanan.

- [ ] The black buffalo is perhaps the most ferocious, dangerous animal on earth. He will charge at almost anything that moves.

- [ ] At ninety degrees below zero ice is like stone and snow is like table salt.

- [ ] More than 40 percent of America's grass seed comes from the state of Oregon.

- [ ] The world's record for a day's rainfall is forty-six inches. This occurred July 14-15, 1911, at Baguio on the island of Luzon in the Philippines.

- [ ] More than 75 percent of heart attack victims survive the first attack.

- [ ] Insects suffer from the same kinds of diseases that human beings do.

- [ ] Brood mares recognize their foals by sight and smell.

- [ ] It is possible for a person to become a Jew in religion but not in race.

- [ ] The Chinese had achieved an advanced civilization by 1200, B.C.

- [ ] World War I began with Germany's declaration of war on Russia August 1, 1914.

- [ ] More than 400,000 different items of merchandise are sold in Macy's store in New York City.

- [ ] New Mexico claims 42 percent of the country's uranium reserves.

- [ ] The Arctic tern, a seabird, flies an average of more than twenty-three thousand miles every year.

- [ ] Ted Evans of Surrey, England, was the tallest man in medical history—9 feet, 3 ½ inches.

- [ ] The earliest system as yet discovered for delivering water to cities was built by the Phoenicians.

- [ ] A mother minnow in her prime lays a thousand eggs a year.

- [ ] Pearls were the first gems discovered and used as ornaments in prehistoric times.

- [ ] Scorpions are immune to their own poison, so they cannot commit suicide if cornered, as was once believed.

- [ ] The average number of eclipses in a year is four, two of the sun and two of the moon.

- [ ] From San Francisco to New York City, a word can fly by telephone in a twelfth of a second.

- [ ] The temperature on the moon falls to 116 degrees below zero at night.

- [ ] President Theodore Roosevelt virtually lost the sight of one eye because of a blow he received while boxing in the White House.

- [ ] Father Flanagan's Boys Home was established in December 1917.

- [ ] Birds have no sweat glands. They cool their bodies by means of air sacs and by opening their beaks and vibrating the walls of their throats.

- [ ] America's original gaslight era began in Baltimore, Maryland, in 1816.

- [ ] The first Nobel prizes were awarded in 1901.

- [ ] Rare varieties of hybrid petunia seeds produced at Paonia, Colorado, sell for as much as seven thousand dollars per pound wholesale.

- [ ] Aristarchus, a Greek who lived from 310 to 250 B.C., was the first to proclaim that the sun stands still and the earth revolves around it.

- [ ] The weasel is a very sound sleeper. It can often be taken up by the head, feet, or tail and swung around for a considerable time before it begins to awaken.

- [ ] Of all substances, helium has the lowest boiling point.

- [ ] About five million Americans enjoy the game of horseshoe pitching each summer.

- [ ] Andrew Jackson once said he was "not fit" to be president of the United States.

- [ ] Today, New York City has many more skyscrapers than any other city in the world.

- [ ] Palm trees live from sixty to one hundred years.

- [ ] Together the United States and Canada produce about one seventh of the world's wool.

- [ ] Brown sugar is sugar from which all the molasses has been removed.

- [ ] A tiger usually will not harm humans unless he is very hungry.

- [ ] The word most frequently used in everyday conversation is *I*.

- [ ] In 1896, J. J. Thomson, of the Cavendish Laboratory at Cambridge University, announced his discovery of electrons.

- [ ] Cherry County, Nebraska, is nearly as large as the states of Connecticut and Rhode Island combined.

- [ ] The venom of poisonous snakes lies in muscular sacs in each side of the upper jaw.

- [ ] John Adams was expresident longer than any other man: from March 4, 1801 to July 1826, a period of twenty-five years and four months.

- [ ] The record weight of a mushroom is thirty pounds.

- [ ] Central City in Colorado was known as the "richest square mile on earth" when it was incorporated in 1864.

- [ ] Salt is used for both freezing and melting.

- [ ] It takes three to four tons of rose petals to produce 2 ½ pounds of rose water.

- [ ] During the winter of 1907-8, in Tamarack, California, 884 inches of snow fell.

- [ ] More than seventy tree species are native to Kentucky.

- [ ] The earliest known explosive was black gunpowder, a mixture of powdered charcoal, sulphur, and saltpeter.

- [ ] It cost $100 million to build the Suez Canal.

- [ ] The sky above us contains more than 5 ½ million billion tons of air.
- [ ] The flattened beaks of ducks enable them to shovel their food from the muddy bottoms of streams.
- [ ] When Empress Elizabeth of Imperial Russia died in 1761, her closets contained fifteen thousand dresses.
- [ ] The first American woolen mill was erected at Rowley, Massachusetts, in 1644.
- [ ] President William McKinley was shot at Buffalo, New York, on September 6, 1901, and died September 14.
- [ ] The first refrigerated railroad car was developed in 1872.
- [ ] Most of the 2,279,843 miles of telegraph wire in the United States are along the railroads.
- [ ] "Babe" Didrickson, famous woman athlete, once threw a baseball 296 feet—a record distance for a woman.
- [ ] The center of population in the United States, according to the 1970 census, is located on the farm of Lawrence B. Friederick, near Mascoutah, Illinois.
- [ ] At certain times, the abdomen of the female lobster is covered with hundreds of eggs.
- [ ] The "Little Church Around the Corner" is a small Protestant Episcopal Church at No. 1, West Twenty-ninth Street in New York City.
- [ ] At birth some blue whale calves are twenty feet long and weigh five thousand pounds.
- [ ] To "sow wild oats" means to commit youthful excesses, to spend one's youth in dissipation.
- [ ] The word *paper* comes from the Egyptian reed papyrus.
- [ ] Boys do not survive the diseases and dangers of childhood as well as girls do.
- [ ] "Fighting Joe Wheeler," owing to illness, went into the battle of Santiago in an ambulance, but when things were going wrong, he got out, mounted his horse, and led a charge up San Juan Hill.
- [ ] The green fat of the turtle is considered particularly delicious.
- [ ] More salt is present in the Atlantic than in the Pacific Ocean.
- [ ] The human body contains about ten trillion cells.
- [ ] A tarantula may live as long as thirty years, taking eight to ten years to mature.
- [ ] New York City was founded by the Dutch, who called it New Amsterdam.
- [ ] Each year more than a million people visit the Statue of Liberty.
- [ ] Louisiana gardeners harvest vegetables even in November.

- [ ] On May 1, 1908, 2.47 inches of rain fell in three minutes in Portobelo, Panama.
- [ ] The rattlesnake sheds its skin three or four times a year, usually three.
- [ ] William Howard Taft was the first president of the United States to play golf. He was regarded as a good player.
- [ ] About 10 percent of the world's population is left-handed.
- [ ] French is the official diplomatic language of the world.
- [ ] Mercury is the only metal that is liquid at room temperature.
- [ ] The Caspian Sea is a lake—not a sea.
- [ ] Nearly half of the nation's peppermint is grown in Oregon.
- [ ] Drownings, rather than high winds, account for most hurricane fatalities.
- [ ] The greatest single block of marble is the fifty-ton slab over the Tomb of the Unknown Soldier at Arlington, Virginia.
- [ ] Nearly all spiders have eight eyes, though they may differ in size and position.
- [ ] The longest recorded interval between the birth of twins was 136 days.
- [ ] San Juan Capistrano, the mission of the swallows, was founded in 1776.
- [ ] In the United States the food harvest from one of every four acres is exported.
- [ ] Chemically salt is known as sodium chloride.
- [ ] Mexico City is 7,434 feet above sea level.
- [ ] About one out of every eighty-five pregnancies terminates in the birth of twins.
- [ ] One horsepower is the power required to lift thirty-three thousand pounds one foot in one minute.
- [ ] There is no law requiring justices of the Supreme Court to be lawyers.
- [ ] The speed of a homing pigeon in still air is thirty to forty miles an hour.
- [ ] Vanilla, in its natural state, is a long green bean.
- [ ] At least ten countries use the eagle as the symbol of supremacy.
- [ ] England's king is not allowed to enter the House of Commons.
- [ ] The average temperature in California's Death Valley in July is 102 degrees.
- [ ] Tin cans contain about 90 percent steel.
- [ ] The finest sponges come from the Mediterranean and Red seas.

- [ ] In Dallas, Texas, if a barking dog disturbs the neighbors, it is considered a misdemeanor.
- [ ] Chemically, corn sugar is the same as cane and beet sugar.
- [ ] Identical twins always have the same color eyes.
- [ ] About 3 ½ billion pounds of wool is produced in the world each year.
- [ ] President Franklin Pierce was a heavy drinker. He did not stop drinking entirely until he formally joined the Episcopal Church about two years before he died.
- [ ] Denver, Colorado, was founded primarily by gold seekers in 1858.
- [ ] The nation's two largest canned Chinese food producers are located in Ohio.
- [ ] Horace Mann is the father of the American public school system.
- [ ] Political poet, John Trumbull, passed the entrance examination to Yale University at age seven.
- [ ] In Berkley, West Virginia, visitors may be guided through an actual coal mine.
- [ ] A maple tree gives the most sap when it is thirty to forty years old.
- [ ] Each year the residents of the United States spend nearly 300 million recreation days in the sport of hunting.
- [ ] There are at least eight species of sea eagles.
- [ ] The chief executive of all the federal prisons is the attorney general.
- [ ] One out of eight office dictionaries are more than twenty years old.
- [ ] The New Testament has been translated into 329 languages.
- [ ] About one-tenth of the earth's surface is permanently covered with ice.
- [ ] William Howard Taft was the first United States president to receive a salary of $75,000 a year.
- [ ] One quintillion is written, 1,000,000,000,000,000,000.
- [ ] The largest salt mine in the world is at Wieliczka, Poland.
- [ ] King Louis X of France played tennis with such abandon that he caught a chill and died.
- [ ] The anaconda snake kills its prey by squeezing.
- [ ] John Adams was the first United States ambassador to England.
- [ ] Jack Dempsy held the heavyweight boxing crown for seven years.
- [ ] The Baltimore and Ohio Railroad once used a horse-drawn locomotive.
- [ ] The anatomy of a frog is such that it must close its eyes to swallow, and if its mouth is held open too long it will suffocate.
- [ ] There is no *u* in the Latin alphabet.

- [ ] The Statue of Liberty was erected in 1886.
- [ ] The average Amercan eats more than seven pounds of pickles a year.
- [ ] Saccharin is derived from coal tar.
- [ ] Holland is largely a Protestant country.
- [ ] In the United States one automobile engine may discharge up to a ton of pollutants into the air annually.
- [ ] Israel has eighteen plants that produce eighteen hundred tons of sesame paste annually for the candy industry.
- [ ] In 1846, California's flag of independence was made in part with a piece of red flannel from a woman's petticoat!
- [ ] Johnny Vander Meer is the only pitcher to hurl two successive no-hit, no-run games in the major league.
- [ ] Seventy percent of the people in the United States live in 2 percent of the total land area of the country.
- [ ] Oil wells in Israel produce 200,000 tons of oil annually.
- [ ] One cocoa bean pod generally yields from twenty to forty cocoa beans.
- [ ] Eastern Michigan University has a course in glassblowing.
- [ ] In certain breeds of sheep, extra fat is stored in the tail.
- [ ] George Washington Carver, one-time slave, developed more than three hundred products from peanuts.
- [ ] Snakes cannot be charmed by music because they have no ears with which to hear.
- [ ] The Lincoln Memorial and the Tomb of the Unknown Soldier are constructed of Colorado white marble.
- [ ] It is illegal to arrest Congressmen for traffic violations.
- [ ] Alcoholism is responsible for more loss of time to industry than all illnesses combined.
- [ ] There are forty-nine different kinds of food mentioned in the Bible.
- [ ] The first steam-driven train in the United States traveled from Albany to Schenectady, New York, on August 9, 1831.
- [ ] A grasshopper's sense of hearing is centered in its front knees.
- [ ] Pure gold is twenty-four carat fine.
- [ ] Zachary Taylor, twelfth president of the United States, never voted in his life, although he was consitutionally eligible to vote in ten presidential elections from 1808 to 1848.
- [ ] The American eel is the only fish that lives and grows in fresh water but goes into the ocean to spawn.
- [ ] Bluefield, West Virginia, is called the air-conditioned city because of its height.

- [ ] The Smithsonian Institution in Washington, D.C. was established August 10, 1846.

- [ ] Parrots have no wishbones.

- [ ] Life expectancy in the United States in 1900 was 47.3 years.

- [ ] In the early days coffee was considered a cure for almost any type of ailment.

- [ ] There are nearly three hundred different oak trees, of which about fifty are native to America.

- [ ] The South Pole was reached by Amundsen on December 14, 1911.

- [ ] About one-third of the population of the United States live in rural areas.

- [ ] The state tree of Colorado is the blue spruce.

- [ ] Utah has more than eighty natural bridges formed by the erosion of wind and water upon sandstone.

- [ ] The neck of the giraffe contains only seven vertebrae. The flexible necks of birds contain fourteen vertebrae.

- [ ] So far as scientists have been able to determine, Iceland had no prehistoric inhabitants.

- [ ] A furlong is equivalent to one-eighth of an English mile.

- [ ] Commercial aviation began in Oklahoma in 1928 when T. E. Braniff organized the Tulsa Oklahoma City Airline.

- [ ] Birds have a poor sense of smell but their eyesight is superior to that of human beings.

- [ ] The wife of President James K. Polk abolished dancing at White House parties.

- [ ] Wheels stopped rolling on the old Santa Fe Trail around 1880.

- [ ] The first Kentucky Derby race was on May 17, 1875.

- [ ] A snake will swallow glass or porcelain eggs as readily as it will real eggs.

- [ ] Yellowstone National Park's Steamboat Geyser, considered the largest in the world, erupts as high as three hundred feet.

- [ ] The custom of putting copper coins on the eyes of the dead originated in England.

- [ ] Cement and concrete are not synonymous. Cement is merely one of the several ingredients of concrete.

- [ ] There are about a hundred species of hawks.

- [ ] Former presidents William Howard Taft, Woodrow Wilson, Calvin Coolidge, and future president Herbert Hoover attended the funeral of President Warren G. Harding in 1923.

- [ ] A typical heavy London fog contains 820,000 dust particles to the cubic inch.

- [ ] Monaco is visited by as many as 1½ million tourists annually.
- [ ] Half of the world's telephones are in North America.
- [ ] During 1816, in several northern states, there were frosts and snow in every month.
- [ ] The common housefly has five eyes located on the upper front part of the head.
- [ ] George Washington operated a brew house for making "small beer" at Mount Vernon.
- [ ] The highest and lowest points in the contiguous United States are within one hundred miles of each other in Inyo County, California.
- [ ] Raccoons in captivity have been known to live more than ten years.
- [ ] A baseball bat must not exceed 2¼ inches in its thickest part.
- [ ] The temperature of an ordinary hen's body is about 107 degrees Fahrenheit.
- [ ] A ham generally weighs 7 percent of the weight of the live hog.
- [ ] Unsightly black heel marks on your kithcen floor can be rubbed out with a pencil eraser.
- [ ] The "bloody" sweat that protects the hippopotamus from the air while out of water, contains no blood.
- [ ] It is unlawful to sell liquor on Indian reservations, or to give it to Indians.
- [ ] The Tremont Hotel in Boston, opened in 1828, introduced the novelty of having a lock on the door of every guest room, no two of which could be opened with the same key. These locks were large and clumsy.
- [ ] A baby elephant weighing two hundred pounds has a trunk only ten or fifteen inches long.
- [ ] The smallest known species of fish in the world reaches an average length of three-eighths of an inch and a maximum length of seven-sixteenths of an inch. These fish are about the size of an ant.
- [ ] When the London barbers were incorporated in 1461, they were the only persons practicing surgery in the city.
- [ ] Noah Webster began writing his famous dictionary in 1807 and finished it in 1828.
- [ ] The late William II of Germany was born with a withered left arm, which surgery and medicine were powerless to remedy.
- [ ] Free-lance writers are persons who write on their own and not as members of the staff of any publication.
- [ ] Lake Erie is the most polluted of America's Great Lakes.
- [ ] It is a well-known fact that thoroughbred horses often form close attachments to goats.
- [ ] By avoirdupois weight, there are seven thousand grains in a pound.

- [ ] The two-dollar bill was the only common United States paper money not counterfeited by Nazi Germany.

- [ ] Colorado's Grand Mesa, near Junction City, has more than two hundred lakes that are two miles above sea level.

- [ ] The Gregorian calendar was introduced by Pope Gregory in A.D. 1582 and was adopted by Great Britain and the English colonies in 1752.

- [ ] A large porcupine may contain as many as thirty-five thousand quills scattered among the hair.

- [ ] Mosquitoes prefer children to adults, and blonds to brunets.

- [ ] Elephants have good memories and sometimes form strong dislikes toward certain people.

- [ ] On the average, 106 boys are born to every 100 girls.

- [ ] Most of the ocean waves described as "mountain high" are really only thirty to forty feet in height.

- [ ] A wild, rash, heedless, foolish, volatile, or giddy person is said to be "harebrained."

- [ ] The heart of a snake has been known to beat twenty-four hours after the head was severed from the body.

- [ ] Fat persons have relatively less blood per pound than lean ones.

- [ ] The distance of the sun from the earth has no bearing upon winter and summer. The sun is farthest from the earth in summer and closest in winter.

- [ ] Chicago annually burns 1½ million tons of coal for heating, and another 6 million tons to generate electricity.

- [ ] The common belief that a drowning person will always rise three times before finally sinking has no scientific foundation.

- [ ] Deers have livers but no organ that takes the place of the gall-bladders in other animals.

- [ ] The skin on the eyelids of a human being is only one-fiftieth of an inch thick.

- [ ] Every four years the calendar is about twenty-four hours behind the astronomical or true solar year.

- [ ] The twinkling of stars is entirely an atmospheric illusion and does not originate with the stars themselves.

- [ ] No animal or bird bleeds well if it is killed in an excited or over-heated condition.

- [ ] There are many species of catfish, some of which grow to be over ten feet long while others attain only a few inches at full growth.

- [ ] It was Aristotle who theorized that without a medium of propagation man would not hear sound.

- [ ] In 1961 the name of the city Stalingrad was changed to Volgograd.

- [ ] Dry ice does not melt in the ordinary sense of the term, but goes directly from a solid to a vapor.
- [ ] The "Dark Ages" as applied to a period of European history is a popular term without specific meaning.
- [ ] On October 24, 1939, women's hosiery made of nylon were placed on sale for the first time in Wilmington, Delaware.
- [ ] The average person in Switzerland eats about eighteen pounds of cheese each year.
- [ ] About 190 different species of oysters are known to science.
- [ ] In a legal sense, only married persons can commit adultery.
- [ ] It takes three pounds of fresh figs to make one pound of dried.
- [ ] At least three-fourths of a mutilated item of United States currency—bill, note, or certificate—must be available in order to redeem it at face value by the United States Treasury.
- [ ] What life is, no man has fathomed. It has neither weight nor demensions, but it does have force.
- [ ] Edwin C. Buxbaum, of Wilmington, Delaware, has more than fifty thousand copies of *National Geographic*.
- [ ] Trees can be measured from large scale aerial photographs to within three feet of their actual height.
- [ ] Nearly every organ in the human body can be kept functioning by a machine.
- [ ] All bears swim readily, occasionally five miles at a time. In hot weather they swim just to cool off.
- [ ] Texas covers 267,399 miles—an area equal to all of New England, plus New York, New Jersey, Pennsylvania, Ohio, and Illinois.
- [ ] Indio, California, is called "The Date Capital of the United States."
- [ ] Fish with forked tails are the fastest swimmers.
- [ ] One out of every four Americans participates in boating.
- [ ] Many of the earliest discoveries of oil and gas wells in Texas were accidental, resulting from drilling for water.
- [ ] The sun, source of all life on earth, has a surface temperature of twelve thousand degrees Fahrenheit.
- [ ] Hair is the least destructible part of the human body. It remains well preserved long after the bony structure has turned to powder.
- [ ] A baby snake gets out of its egg by means of a temporary egg tooth, as a chick does.
- [ ] The Liberty Bell, which cracked in 1835 as it was being tolled for the funeral of Chief Justice John Marshall, cracked beyond repair as it was being rung on Washington's Birthday in 1846.
- [ ] The *Graf Zeppelin* was the only airship to fly completely around the world.

- [ ] The planet Jupiter is more than fourteen times larger than the earth.
- [ ] There is a recipe in the Bible for making friends. See Proverbs 18:24.
- [ ] The Federal Bureau of Investigation had its beginning in 1908.
- [ ] There are at least eleven species of the palm tree.
- [ ] There are about two thousand varieties of shrimp.
- [ ] Mexico's silver mines are the most productive in the world.
- [ ] There is no proof that Barnum once said, "There is a sucker born every minute."
- [ ] Saint Patrick was not an Irishman. He was born in Britain.
- [ ] Oaks are usually the last trees in the forest to shed their leaves.
- [ ] The first state gasoline tax was imposed in Oklahoma by the legislature in 1924.
- [ ] Feeble-minded people are divided into three classes: idiots, imbeciles, and morons.
- [ ] A person who has six fingers or six toes on one or both of his hands or feet is said to be afflicted with hexadactylism.
- [ ] Andrew Jackson was the first president of the United States to be married to a divorcee.
- [ ] The albatross is an exceedingly large and strong seabird. Specimens with a wingspread of up to seventeen feet have been known.
- [ ] The cormorant can swim just as fast as it can fly.
- [ ] Being overweight can shorten the life of an American adult by about 5½ years.
- [ ] President Franklin D. Roosevelt vetoed 631 bills during his four terms in office.
- [ ] Condors with a wingspread of nine feet have been known.
- [ ] Only in bright sunshine are white clothes materially cooler than dark clothes.
- [ ] Nearly half the nation's peppermint is grown in Oregon.
- [ ] Almost one-half of the women in the United States between the ages of eighteen and sixty-four work outside the home.
- [ ] Mount Everest is the highest mountain in the world.
- [ ] Matthew Alexander Henson, a Negro, was the only American to accompany Peary to the North Pole. He helped to plant the American flag there on April 6, 1901.
- [ ] Baseball bats are made of ash.
- [ ] Charles III of France was called "Charles the Simple."
- [ ] The sweet gum tree is also known as the liquid-ambar.

- [ ] The Chisholm Trail was named after the Scotch-Cherokee trader Jesse Chisholm, who lived from 1806 to 1868.

- [ ] During their preschool years, children learn the most about the properties of the world in which he lives by playing.

- [ ] Christian Endeavor was organized by Rev. Francis Edward Clark of the Congregational Church in Portland, Maine, in 1881.

- [ ] The chameleon depends more on his vision than he does on his sense of smell.

- [ ] At the time of the Great London Fire in September 1666, London covered 375 acres. Only 75 of these acres came out unscathed.

- [ ] The name "Cajuns" is derived from "Acadians" and it refers to the descendants of the French Canadians who found their way to southern Louisiana after they had been expelled by the British because they would not swear allegiance to the British crown.

- [ ] Spring tide occurs at full and new moon when the sun and moon are in a straight line with the earth.

- [ ] The completion of the railroads contributed greatly to the decline of the canals which were built during the nineteenth century.